STEVEN G. KAUTNER

ANNA'S STORY

A TRUE STORY OF A YOUNG GIRL'S WILL TO SURVIVE IN THE AFTERMATH OF WORLD WAR II

STEVEN G. KAUTNER

STEVEN G. KAUTNER

First originally published by Newman Springs Publishing 2022

978-1-969367-24-3 Paperback

978-1-969367-25-0 Hardback

978-1-969367-26-7 Digital online

Printed in the United States of America

Foreword

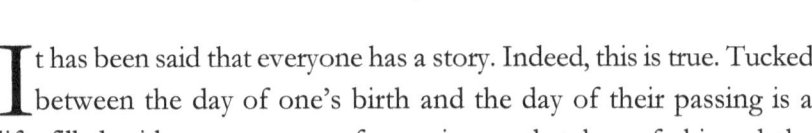

It has been said that everyone has a story. Indeed, this is true. Tucked between the day of one's birth and the day of their passing is a life filled with a vast array of experiences that have fashioned the person into who they are today.

In our passing acquaintances, we are rarely afforded the opportunity to learn much about the person we have met. We often say our goodbyes without truly knowing each other. Seldom, if ever, will we inquire by asking someone to tell us their story. I have often reflected upon how much we are likely missing by failing to take the time to do this.

On several occasions over the years, I have had the joy of doing just this; and I must admit, more often than not, I have heard some amazing stories. I have even said to a few, "You need to write a book!"

What you now hold in your hands is just that—a story that needed to become a book.

I met Anna Berry, the main character in this book, in 2000, in Ormond Beach, Florida. Anna and her husband had just relocated from West Palm Beach. Shortly following our being introduced to each other, my conversations with the knowledge of this dear person became increasingly intriguing. Every time we would talk, Anna's story revealed more and more of the history behind this person. Her post-WWII childhood and all the events to follow captured my attention and imagination. It has been over two decades since we first met, and since that time, her story has been in progress.

Anna would frequently express her desire to put her story into print. It was a dream she has held for a long time. Her hopes have been that others who read it will be enriched and encouraged that, regardless of how difficult life may be at any time, one would never lose heart. Anna exemplifies this.

The vivid descriptions of things Anna witnessed and endured as a young child, written on these pages, rival a Hollywood script—and they are true. What you are about to read, Anna has lived. Anna's post-WWII childhood following the defeat of Hitler and his Nazi regime and the events that followed in an occupied Germany and its surrounding region will likely astonish you. I felt at times, as I read the manuscript, that I was there with her and that I knew this little girl and was witnessing her growing up into a mature woman.

The story is filled with joys and sorrows, as well as gains and losses. In them all, one thing will become increasingly obvious to you—Anna's resilient nature, determination, and bright disposition, even in some of the most challenging circumstances. Anna has always maintained hope. These are the things that have sustained her.

However, in retrospect, there is one key ingredient to all this that came later in her life. Anna attributes her perseverance to her Christian faith.

Anna became a Christian later in life, but this has not in any way hindered her conviction that all things that came before were leading up to this event. Things seemed to make sense to her after coming to faith. She saw God's providence and preservation in all she has endured. If there is anything she wants to communicate in telling us her story, this is it.

STEVEN G. KAUTNER

I want to personally thank the author, Steven G. Kautner, who is Anna's son, for his labor of love in putting his mom's personal notes and conversations into print. This has been a lengthy and arduous task.

Acknowledgments

First and foremost, I wish to acknowledge my mother, Anna, whose unrelenting determination to get this story told was my inspiration to write this book. Almost equally as important to this process was my wife, Varida Kautner. She was my editor, spellchecker, grammar checker, listener, and all-around best friend. She believed in my writ- ing ability more than I did.

The other people I would like to honor are the thousands of ethnic Germans who lived this nightmare, including many of my own family members. They fought for their lives, and many of them did not survive. It is to them that I dedicate this book.

I trust you will find what you are about to read as captivating as I did. It is indeed a wonderful story that needed to be told. Enjoy!

Mitch Pridgen Daytona Beach, Florida 2021

Contents

Introduction

What you are about to read is the true story of a young girl named Anna Friedrich, born and raised in East Central Europe by ethnic German parents during and after World War II. The town she lived in was called Setschan, located on the Temesch River in the Banat region of Northern Serbia, then part of Yugoslavia. The Danube River runs along the border between Romania and Serbia. The Banat region is known for its metal ore mining, which brought jobs and industrialization, and for its rich soil, perfect for making a life of farming. The Banat region was also known for its cultural diversity. During the time of this story, the region was populated with Serbs, Croatians, Hungarians, Romanians, Bulgarians, Jews, Gypsies, and ethnic Germans.

Sometime around 1718, the ethnic Germans of the Banat came to be known as Danube Swabian, or *Donauschwaben* in the German language, aptly named for their settlements along the Danube River and because some of the German immigrants were originally associated with the Swabian culture found in Southwestern Germany. Understanding how these ethnic Germans found their way to Yugoslavia is going to require a brief history lesson.

The great Swabian migration

In the early seventeenth century, the land known as Serbia was in Hungary, which was part of the Habsburg Empire of East Central Europe. During this time, the Ottoman Turkish Empire's voracious appetite for land propelled them north through Hungary toward Austria, devouring everything in their path. Serbia was easily swallowed up by the Ottoman Turks. By 1683, the Ottomans were at the gates of Vienna. With the help of German and Polish military forces, the Habsburg military, led by Prince Eugene of Savoy, succeeded in defeating and driving back the Ottoman Turks. By 1718, after numerous military campaigns, the Habsburg Empire was able to claim victory and take back much of the land that had been conquered by the Ottomans. One such region reclaimed by Habsburg was most of Serbia, which included the Banat region.

Most of the land of the Banat region was desolate and uninhabited. There was no infrastructure, no roads, and no bridges, just vast swaths of flat barren land. The area had been decimated by 150 years of Ottoman Turk occupation before they were driven out. The Banat had one thing in its favor: the Danube River and all its tributaries that made the land perfect for farming, or so it seemed. The untamed rivers of the Banat often overflowed due to heavy rainfall, causing floods and enormous areas of swampland.

Starting around 1718, the Habsburg Empire came up with a plan to colonize the land taken back from the Ottoman Turks. An organized settlement program was developed and sponsored by the Habsburg government to accomplish three things: cultivate the land for farming, colonize the areas to prevent further invasion, and promote the Roman Catholic religion. The Habsburgs looked to the Catholic German population living in what is now Western and Southern Germany for volunteers. The Germans were offered enticements such as free land, homesites, building materials, livestock, and tax benefits.

Most of the Germans that chose to emigrate to this new land were second- and third-born sons and not in line to inherit the family farm. It was customary that only firstborn sons would inherit the family property. Any successive sons were expected to make a life of their own elsewhere. From 1718 to 1787, migrations of the Germans occurred in three waves. The first wave of about fifteen thousand Germans left the checkpoint in Vienna and traveled by foot or in caravans of horse-drawn wagons. Huge wooden barges were constructed so immigrants could float down the Danube River to their settlement destination. Once they arrived, the barges were dismantled and used as a building material. The first wave of German settlers endured hardships never before experienced. Not only was the land not as hospitable as they were led to believe, but most of them were killed by rogue Turkish invaders or died from sickness and disease.

The second wave of immigrants occurred between 1744 and 1772. This population of about fifty thousand ethnic Germans was better organized and better equipped. They rebuilt most of the settlements and reestablished the towns built by the first wave. The third wave of about eighty thousand ethnic Germans occurred between 1782 and 1787. With much of the hard work already done by the first and second waves, the third wave of immigrants had the best chances of success.

By 1789, the Habsburg government ended the colonization program. Many more settlers continued to migrate to Southern Hungary without government encouragement, in hopes of finding a better life. The migrations continued until 1829 when the Habsburg government declared that only settlers able to pay five hundred guilders were allowed to migrate. The first Friedrich settlers migrated to the Banat in 1806.

Before the end of the 1800s, more than 1,200 towns were established throughout Southern Hungary, with the highest concentration in the Banat region. Most of the towns had more than 90 percent ethnic German inhabitants. The populations of these towns ranged between one thousand to eight thousand people. German was the primary language. Schools within these towns taught lessons in German. The Catholic Church, located in the center of each town, gave sermons in German. The Swabian population in the Banat region alone grew to over one million.

The ethnic Germans were hardworking, industrious people. Many of the immigrants of the third wave were tradesmen and business owners. It was not long before the Banat region earned the title of Breadbasket of Europe.

Throughout the centuries, the borders and names of countries in Eastern Europe had changed dramatically. The biggest changes to the geographics of the area came just after World War I, which ended in 1918. That year saw the breakup of the Austro-Hungary Kingdom, which included Austria, Hungary, Czechoslovakia, Romania, Serbia, and Bulgaria. A state of union was formed between seven Slavic nations: Serbia, Croatia, Montenegro, Bosnia-Herzegovina, Slovenia, Kosovo, and Macedonia. The union was called the Kingdom of Serbs, Croats, and Slovenes, later to become Yugoslavia. The Banat region was divided between Romania, Hungary, and Yugoslavia.

The town of Setschan, which was originally part of Hungary, was now in Yugoslavian territory. It is not known exactly when Setschan was established as a town although some records date back to around 1800. By 1860, it had a population of about 2,200 people. The town was 92 percent ethnic German, with the remaining 8 per- cent being Serbs, Jews, Hungarians, and Gypsies. The townspeople of Setschan lived in harmony with their ethnic neighbors. The start of World War II would change that part of the world forever.

World War II

World War II has been the subject of countless books, films, plays, magazines, lectures, and much more. History has recorded just about every minute of WWII from beginning to end. In contrast, little is known about what happened after WWII. In particular, what were the effects of the war on the European people that survived?

The aftermath. The end of World War II was the beginning of the horror for many Europeans, especially the ethnic German populations of Eastern Europe. After WWII, countries like Poland, Czechoslovakia, Yugoslavia, and the Soviet Union expelled millions of ethnic Germans living within their borders as retribution for the atrocities perpetrated by the Nazis against their people. These expulsions created the largest forced migration of a population in human history. It was estimated that more than fifteen million ethnic Germans became refugees between 1945 and 1950. Most of them left behind everything they owned and made the long arduous journey, sometimes hundreds of kilometers, many by foot, to Austria and Germany. Many ethnic Germans died along the way from starvation and disease. As chaotic and horrible as this exodus was, these Germans were the lucky ones. The ethnic German families that decided to stay in their homes and fight for their property faced a fate far more horrific than the expulsions.

At the beginning of WWII, Yugoslavia refused to align with the Nazis and instead fought against them. By April 1941, the Royal Yugoslav Army lost the fight and surrendered to the Nazis. The Nazi Germans immediately divided up the country between Germany, Italy, Hungary, and Bulgaria. The Nazis set up garrison outposts, checkpoints, and prison camps. The torture and murder of the Yugoslavian citizens by the Nazis instilled a deep hatred of the Germans—all Germans, including the ethnic German civilians, farmers, tradesmen, and business owners who wanted nothing to do with the war.

The occupation of Yugoslavia by Axis forces (Nazi Germany and its collaborators) did meet some resistance from Chetniks rebels and Serb Partisans although fierce infighting took place between these two groups. The Serbian Partisans were unorganized and undisci- plined until the rise to power of Josip Broz, otherwise known as Tito. Born in Croatia, Tito was a communist and a revolutionary. As the self-appointed leader of the partisans, Tito was very effective at orga- nizing and waging guerrilla warfare against the occupying German Army. The partisans of Yugoslavia adopted the communist ideology and came to be known as Tito Communist Partisans.

By late 1944 throughout Europe, the German Wehrmacht (War Machine) was showing signs of defeat. Taking advantage of the weakening German Army, the Communist Partisans, with the help of the advancing Russian Red Army, succeeded in driving the Nazi German Army and their collaborators out of Yugoslavia. As a result, the Communist Partisans under Tito came to be recognized as a major military force.

Starting in 1945, with permission from Yugoslavian authorities, the Communist Partisans carried out the deportation of over one million Danube Swabians. The Swabian Germans that chose not to leave voluntarily were rounded up at gunpoint by the Communist Partisans and forced into ghettos. After many months of being crowded into small sections of each town, with twenty-five to thirty people in each house, the Swabian Germans were transported by rail-road cattle cars to concentration death camps, set up and guarded by armed Communist Partisan Serbian Soldiers. Starvation and disease were the preferred methods of exterminating the Swabian ethnic Germans.

Such was the fate of the Friedrich family. In 1945, Anna Friedrich was twelve years old. Her father and two brothers, Mischi and Juri, had volunteered to fight for the German Army. This left Mother, forty-one; her oldest child Kathi, twenty-four, with her own child Annemarie, four; and Mother's two youngest children, Anna and Stefan, fourteen, to fend for themselves. What happens next is what this story is about. This is Anna's story told from her experiences and memories.

Map of the former Yugoslavia. The star shows the location of the town of Setschan

Anna's Story

It was mid-January of the year 1940. At six o'clock in the morning, it was still dark outside. Seven-year-old Anna was awoken by the sound of clanging pots and pans coming from the kitchen. Anna's mother was already up preparing breakfast and firing up the oven. The only source of heat in the entire house was a brown brick oven located in the kitchen adjacent to the main bedroom. Mother would bring dried cornstalks and firewood into the house the night before in anticipation of the morning cold. The room Anna slept in was still very cold. She would sometimes test how cold it was by exhaling hard and, with a narrow beam of light escaping from the white curtains on the window of the kitchen door, it was just enough to see how much steam would exit her mouth. It was particularly cold on this winter day; and even the smell of her favorite breakfast, fresh-baked bread and onion soup, could not coax Anna out from under her warm, overstuffed down-filled comforter and pillow.

Anna shared a bed with her mother, while her father slept in his own bed. Anna's nine-year-old brother, Stefan, slept in a small day bed next to the door. Anna could still feel her mother's warmth from the space beside her. She knew that any second now, Mother would be calling her and Stefan to wake up. "Anna, Stefan, aufwachen," Mother called from the kitchen. Still, no movement in Anna's bed. She could hear rustling in the room, followed by the soft pattering of feet. She knew this sound to be Stefan, who was always up before her. She just wasn't ready to throw herself out into that cold air yet. A minute later, Mother called again; this time much more deliberate. "Anna!" She knew that tone to mean, "get up now or else." Anna slid out of her bed and onto a small oval-shaped rug beside her bed on the wooden plank floor. The rug was weaved from strips of cloth rag material. She immediately thought, *This is not so bad.* The air was finally starting to warm up a bit.

Anna's clothes were draped over a wooden chair next to her bed. She quickly pulled her plain blue dress over her head, put on her white apron with lace trim, and sat down on the wooden bench in front of the brick oven wall to put on her gray-and-black thigh-high woolen stockings. She pulled them up as high as she could and secured them with an elastic band. She hated those stockings because they made her itch just like the wool sweater she had to wear. She would soon forget about the itching as she looked at herself in the mirror that was leaning against the wall over a small pine dresser positioned between two windows. She picked up the comb from the dresser and began combing her short, straight light-brown hair, first to one side, then to the other side, finally holding it in place with a hairclip. She hesitated a moment as she stared at her reflection in the mirror. She turned to one side, then to the other side, smiled, and ran into the kitchen.

Anna's mother was standing next to the oven, her gray apron wrapped around her body and a babushka over her head tied under her chin. She wore a long black skirt and a brown blouse. "Hurry, Anna, your soup is getting cold," Mother said. Anna picked up the only pair of shoes she owned from the mat by the front door. Mother had brought them in from outside the night before. She sat down on one of the wooden chairs at the kitchen table to put them on. Stefan already had his shoes on and was sitting at the table, tapping them on the earthen floor, trying to catch his sister's attention. She looked up at him; and he gave her a smirk, the kind she knew all too well that meant, *You will never beat me to the table.*

Anna's soup was already on the table along with a piece of bread. She broke the bread into small pieces and put them in the soup. She slurped up every last morsel of the onion soup and bread and finished with a loud burp. "Nah, Anna!" Mother would say without turning around. Stefan began to laugh out loud when Anna looked at him and gave him a smirk.

Anna moved her chair closer to the source of heat. The heavy cast iron oven door, decorated with blue-and-gray scorch marks, was left open to allow the heat to come into the kitchen and drift into the bedroom. The dried cornstalks from autumn's corn harvest crackled loudly as they burned in the oven. Anna loved that sound and could sit there, mesmerized, in front of the fire for hours.

"Okay, Anna, time to get ready for school," Mother would say in German. The thought of walking almost one kilometer to school in the frigid winter air was not much of an incentive for Anna to jump up out of her chair. Stefan needed no encouragement. He stood up without delay, ran to the front door where his hat and coat hung from a wooden dowel on the wall, and put them on as fast as he could. He stood facing the front door for a moment, fastening the last button of his brown canvas winter coat with tan-and-green-checkered flannel lining. He put on his gray wool knitted hat, one that Oma (Grandmother) knit for him, slipped on his dark-gray woolen mittens, and opened the front door. He was just about to run out when Mother called to him, "Stefan, don't forget to come home right after school."

"Ja, ja, ich weis schon" (Yes, I know). On his way out the door, he turned to Anna; made a face at her, which she quickly returned; and ran out the door. Stefan's best friend, Klosi, lived only a few houses down the street. The two boys would meet up and walk to school together.

Anna stood up and pushed her chair back to the table. Mother was already in the front bedroom, opening the window for fresh air.

She would flip over the feather bed and fluff it up. She fluffed up the down-filled pillows and mattress filled with cornhusks. "The bedroom was just starting to get warm," Anna would say to herself. "Why does Mother have to open the window?"

She quickly ran into the bedroom; grabbed her gray sweater, scarf, and gray knit mittens; and ran back into the kitchen and slowly put them on. Her brown winter coat hung on a wooden dowel next to the front door, just like her brother Stefan's. She put on her coat and buttoned it as she opened the front door. "Bye, Mother," she would say as she ran out the door and headed straight for the outhouse toward the back of the yard. The outhouse was like an icebox inside. She hated sitting on that cold seat. When she was finished, she ran to the street and started her walk to school.

School was exactly twenty-five houses down the street from Anna's home. She knew this because every morning, she would count them to make the time go quicker. The schoolhouse was a huge two-story red-brick building. Numerous brick columns lined the front of the building, all evenly spaced and connected together like a chain, with ornate wrought-iron work. This served as a barrier between the building and the street. The barrier was interrupted at the center of the building with a larger than normal double-door entrance. The classrooms were lined up on each side of the main hallway.

Anna's classroom was on the first floor, right by the school's entrance. Stefan's classroom was on the second floor. School started at eight. Anna would always get there early so she had time to hang up her winter garments and sit down to chat with her friends before class started. The classrooms were made up of boys and girls together. The desks were arranged in rows, pretty much like any typical school classroom. There were a few pictures hanging on the walls. Two that Anna remembered were a picture of Prince Eugene of Savoy on horseback, and directly in front of the classroom on the wall behind the teacher's desk was a picture of Jesus Christ on a cross.

Father Julius Morawetz was a Catholic priest from the only church in the town of Setschan. He was part of the teaching staff although not officially a teacher. He would come to Anna's classroom every Wednesday to teach religion. He was a kind old man with short gray hair, bushy gray eyebrows, and a warm smile. Anna liked him very much. She loved to listen to him speak. He came into the classroom wearing a long black robe, the kind you would expect a Catholic priest to wear.

Anna's teacher was named Frau Grob. She was a middle-aged woman—tall and lean, with short graying hair. She wore a dark-colored midcalf-length dress with knee-high nylon stockings and black leather oxford shoes. Frau Grob was stern but not mean. She loved the children and loved teaching. She taught all the lessons except, of course, religion. Math, science, history, and German language were the primary subjects. All the lessons in Anna's class were taught in German.

Nearly all the students were of German ethnicity while the others were Hungarian, Serbian, and a few children from Gypsy families. Children of all ethnicities were taught together and grouped according to age.

At ten in the morning, the children would get a twenty-minute recess. This was the only time they would be allowed to go to the outhouse. This was also the only time they were allowed to go outside to run and holler and play games. Children from all grades were on the playground at the same time. On cold winter days, the girls would usually be huddled together in groups of similar ages on one side of the playground while boys would do the same on the opposite side. Rarely would they intermingle or even play a game together.

The games they played were the usual children's playground

games: *fussball* (soccer), jump rope, hopscotch. But when it was this cold, they would mostly stand around and scream at each other who's the best and whom can they make fun of. This would sometimes end up in squabbles or even physical fights. When twenty minutes had passed, one of the teachers would get bundled up, put her boots on, march outside, and blow a loud whistle, signaling to the children that recess was over and it was time to go back to class.

The boys and girls would form lines according to classes before being led by the teacher back into the classrooms. While outside, discipline was somewhat lax, so the children were constantly push-ing and shoving and yelling at each other. While in class, they were mostly well-behaved. As you might expect, there always seemed to be one class clown in every schoolroom. In Anna's classroom, his name was Sepp. He would drink the black ink from the ink jar found at every desk and then stick his black tongue out at everyone, making them laugh hysterically.

At twelve o'clock, the lunch bell would sound. By then, the children were starving, so the most important thing to them was being the first one out the door. All the children went home to eat lunch, with some having a much longer walk than others. To accom-modate them, the lunch period was two hours long. For Anna, lunch was quick and simple. She would get a piece of bread with lard, salt, and pepper, or bread with homemade jam. Stefan would also come home for lunch, and sometimes, they would both eat leftovers from the previous night's dinner. Just before two in the afternoon, it was back to school for afternoon classes until four.

After-school chores

Anna would go straight home after school. This was her time to do chores around the house. Bringing water from the well, feeding the chickens, and gathering eggs from the chicken coup were the majority of her chores. After she finished those, she was allowed to go outside and play for a while, but in winter, she preferred to stay indoors. "What are we having for dinner, Mother? Sure smells good," Anna said as she came in from feeding the chickens.

"First, take off your shoes and coat and leave your shoes outside," Mother said. "You will find out when it is put on the table." Anna hung up her coat on the wooden peg by the door and placed her shoes just outside the front door. She poured some water into the washbowl located on a small wooden table next to the front door. She washed her hands and face and then poured the used water into the bucket below the washbowl table.

"Where is Stefan? Why isn't he home yet?" Anna asked. "Don't worry about Stefan. He'll be home soon," Mother said. "Is Father going to come home tonight?" Anna asked.

"Ja, ja, he is coming home," Mother answered.

"I hope he doesn't have to practice music," Anna said. "Maybe he will play a game with us."

Anna's father, Stefan, did not come home every evening. Neither did her three older siblings: Kathi, Mischi, and Juri. It was common for the working class to sleep at the jobsite and only go home on weekends. They would sometimes travel long distances to get to work, and because their only mode of transportation was by foot or bicycle, it was not very practical to travel home every day, especially at night in the dark and in the middle of winter. The roads were not lighted very well—most of them, not at all. This made the roads dangerous to use at night, not to mention scary. Only a few people in Setschan were wealthy enough to afford their own automobiles. Livelihood in the region was primarily farming. A farmer would get much more use out of a farm tractor than an automobile. Horse and buggy was a popular method of transportation. The Friedrich family did not own a horse or a buggy.

Anna's father worked mostly in the construction trades. His specialty was bricklaying, but he also did many odd jobs. In the winter, when construction jobs stopped or slowed down to a crawl, Father would work as a chimney sweeper. Mischi sometimes worked with Father in construction. Juri worked as a farmhand on a nearby farm. Juri hated construction work, and so his only other choice was to work on a farm. Father decided to teach his son a lesson. He made a deal with a local farm owner, one he knew to be mean and crotchety. The deal was that the old farmer would take Juri on as a farm helper, mostly shoveling manure and cleaning out stalls. This was the kind of work that Father hoped Juri would learn to hate. His plan backfired because the old farmer grew quite fond of Juri and soon treated him like his own son. Juri was promoted to animal caretaker, a job he loved.

Anna's sister, Kathi, was the oldest of the five siblings. At nineteen years old, she had already moved into the home of her employer, a wealthy family, where she worked as a housemaid. Kathi was dedicated to her job, but her dream was to get married and raise a family of her own. She came home only on Sundays.

It was already dark outside when Father came home from working all day as a chimney sweep. He had taken off his dirty work coat and hat and plopped down on one of the kitchen chairs. "Nah, Stefan, you're filthy! Go wash up before you sit down," Mother said. The moment Anna saw his face, she began to laugh out loud. His face was completely black from chimney soot, except for a perfect line across the middle of his forehead where his hat had protected him from falling soot.

Stefan finally came home as Father was washing his face and

hands in the washbowl. Ordinarily, the men of the house didn't mind using the same water to wash, but when Stefan looked into the washbowl, the water was black from chimney soot. Stefan quickly emptied the washbowl and poured fresh water from the water pitcher.

Soon, the family was ready to sit down at the kitchen table for dinner. Tonight's dinner was *kartoffel* (potato) goulash with a slice of fresh bread. Meals were mostly of German fare, and during the winter months, Mother always prepared and served them hot. During the week, meals were simple and made with vegetables and fruits from the garden. They also ate fresh eggs and sometimes meat, mostly smoked pork and occasionally chicken. On special occasions, such as Christmas or Easter, Mother would purchase a live goose or sometimes a duck from a local farmer, then slaughter and cook it. This was considered a feast.

Mother stayed home every day and ran the household. During the growing season, from early spring to late autumn, she kept very busy tending to the vegetable garden. They grew a variety of vegetables along with fresh fruit from the numerous fruit trees on their property. With careful planning, they would have enough produce for the entire year. What they did not eat during the summer months would be preserved in glass jars for consumption during the winter.

Behind the garden, in line with a large mulberry tree, were the animal pens. Mother raised chickens, ducks, pigs, and sometimes rabbits. Tending to the chickens was mostly Anna's job. She would feed them a mixture of dry corn and grain every day. Pigs were raised mostly for meat and lard. In the pigsty, one pig was kept in a stall, separate from the rest. The lone pig would be fattened up as much as possible. It was not allowed to run around the pen so as to prevent it from burning off fat. It would be slaughtered mostly for its lard along with three or four other pigs. This will be explained later.

The ducks were plucked for their feathers, and the down was used to stuff pillows and comforters. This process didn't harm the fowl, but that did not keep them from ferociously fighting back. Some of the ducks were fattened up and butchered for special occasions.

Father's passion

After the Sunday meal, Father, Mischi, and Juri would don their uniforms and polish the brass of their instruments in preparation for an afternoon of playing music, dancing, and singing. Father and his two sons—along with Grandfather (Opa) Jacob Friedrich, who was the band leader; uncles; and cousins—were all members of a brass band called the Draxler Band. Opa Friedrich was also one of the most musically talented of the band members. He was able to play every type of instrument used in the band. In fact, he taught all the band members how to play.

The band would play mostly German-inspired music like waltzes, polkas, Zepler, and Landlers. Another name for this kind of band was oompah-pah. A popular misconception these days is that they played mostly beer-drinking songs. Father played the clarinet, Mischi played the trumpet, and Juri played the tuba. The band played for just about any occasion, including weddings, funerals, christenings, and birthdays. Opa would turn no invitation down.

The festivities on Sundays started around two in the afternoon. The band played at the Weber's Music Hall, which was walking distance from home. Father and his sons would leave early for Weber's Hall, while the girls would get ready. On Sundays, Kathi would come home. Shoes would be polished the day before. Kathi would put on her best dress, a royal-blue skirt-and-blouse combo with a black silky embroidered shawl to top it off.

Mother combed Kathi's hair, braided it into a ponytail, and

rolled it into a bun on top of her head, which was held in place with a large comb. Anna would sit and watch this process in awe, hoping someday she would be as beautiful as Kathi. At nineteen, Kathi was one of the prettiest young ladies in town. She would walk to Weber's alone; or her boyfriend, Stefan Latzkowitsch, would pick her up and they would walk together arm in arm.

Mother put on her best Sunday dress. She stood in front of the mirror with her brown eyes and long, slightly wavy brown hair which, like Kathi's, was braided and rolled up on top of her head in a bun and held in place with large hair pins instead of a comb. Anna thought she was the prettiest Mother in town. Anna sat, mesmerized, watching her Mother get ready. "Come on, Anna. Get dressed," Mother would say. Just before they left for Weber Hall, Mother sat Anna down and made her promise to be on her best behavior. "No running around and no yelling," Mother said to Anna in her most serious tone.

"Ja, ja, I promise," Anna would say to Mother.

Anna and Mother walked hand in hand to Weber Hall. Anna was so excited, she could hardly contain herself. The closer they got, the louder the music was. Anna would be jumping and singing. "Anna, don't forget you promised," Mother said.

"I can hear Father playing," Anna would say. The admission to get into Weber Hall was around four dinar for boys. Girls were admitted for free. Once they got there, Anna and Mother would enter through the side gate.

Inside the dance hall, wooden benches lined the walls on each side of the dance floor. Sitting there were mothers, grandmothers, aunts, and children. They would be tapping their feet to the music and gossiping—"Oh look, Peter is dancing with Maria," someone would say, or, "Why is nobody dancing with my daughter?"

At one end of the hall were tables and chairs. The men and boys would sit around the tables. The men drank draft beer or wine; the boys would drink soda. Family members of the band were also seated at one of the tables. The young girls of the town would stand around on the sidelines, hoping some nice boy would ask them to dance. Father's youngest brother, Mischko, who was also in the band, sat at the table with his wife, Anna, next to Mother.

Mother's oldest brother Georg was there with his wife, Nanschi, along with their daughter Anna and ten-year-old son Johann, who had Down syndrome. Uncle Georg would often ask Mother to dance. Anna's oldest brother Mischi would take a break from playing his instrument just to dance with Mother. He loved dancing with a passion. Men would often whoop and yahoo loudly while danc- ing. Girls would be spun around by their dance partners until their dresses would fly up.

Anna was having a hard time keeping her promise to Mother. She would practice dance steps with the other girls her age. She had so much pent-up energy that she just wanted to run. Soon, she couldn't hold back any longer. She started running with her friends in one door and out the other. She ran past Mother, close enough for Mother to grab her arm. "That's enough now. Sit down by me and watch," Mother said, knowing that Anna would eventually break her promise.

She bought Anna a bottle of Sprudel, a flavored club soda. She soon settled down and turned her attention to the dance floor. She watched the couples lock arms and twirl. "Look, there's Kathi and Stefan," Anna said. Kathi smiled at Anna as she twirled by. Anna could feel the wind from her flying skirt as her sister passed. The children would often reach out and touch the skirts as they flew by. When the band played the Zepler, everyone would step aside to give the dance floor to Kathi and Stefan Latzkowitsch. Father would stand while he played his clarinet as he watched his daughter dance. He was so proud of her.

Winter

The winters in Setschan were not severe but cold enough to spend most days at home, indoors, when not at school. Anna remembers being alone with Mother while sitting on the wooden bench in the front bedroom next to the brick wall of the oven and learning how to knit. First, a scarf, then mittens, then stockings, using five needles. She remembers those quiet times, with no distractions, just the two of them, talking and knitting.

Mother was so patient, taking the time to show Anna all the little nuances of knitting. She would draw a bird or a flower on a piece of white cloth and then show Anna how to embroider. Anna loved the beautiful colors of embroidery thread; they were like a treasure to her. Some days, Mother would bring out her *spinnrad* (spinning loom) to teach Anna how to spin her own yarn. She remembered holding a stick with lamb's wool wrapped around it while Mother would operate the foot pedal that made the wheel turn. Mother pulled the wool slowly from the stick while the loom would twist it into yarn. Anna often thought that after having three boys, Mother enjoyed having another girl around. She would smile and nod her head at Anna. That was her way of saying I love you.

Anna's friend Nani Focht lived just a few houses down the street. She would come over to Anna's house with her homemade sled. They would pull each other around or slide down a small hill near Anna's house. Nani had lots of freckles and long black hair, parted down the middle with two pigtails. On some weekends, they would go skating. During the winter months, a small stream across the street from Anna's Oma Rech's house would overflow to form a pond; and when the temperature became cold enough, the pond would freeze, creating a perfect skating rink. Neither of the girls had ice skates but had just as much fun sliding around with their shoes. When they reached their limit of fun and exhaustion, they would walk over to Oma's house to warm up a little before the walk home. They both knew that there was a good chance that Oma would give them some strudel or hot cocoa.

Spring

The temperature outside was slowly getting warmer as spring approached. There was much to do in preparation for the growing seasons. Mother prepared two nests in the house attic, one for each of the two hens she would select. Bricks were used to form two square boxes, which were then filled with straw. Mother would then bring in the two hens and as many eggs as she could find. The hens would stay in the nests until the eggs hatched. After the eggs hatched, Mother brought the hens and their chicks down from the attic and into the front yard to keep them away from the other chickens in the backyard.

Wednesday nights, Mother prepared dough for making bread the next day. She had on a plain white blouse with the sleeves rolled up and a half apron over her long skirt. She wore a babushka over her head, tied under her chin. Anna watched from her bed as Mother kneaded the dough with her hands until pearls of sweat would form on her forehead. She remembers her excitement in anticipation of fresh warm bread the following day.

Kathi's engagement

Around the end of March 1940, Kathi announced that she would be getting married to Stefan Latzkowitsch. Anna was so excited to hear that her sister was engaged to be married. She was the first of all the cousins and brothers to be married. Mother and Father were not happy with Kathi's choice of husband. Stefan Latzkowitsch had no means of support, no viable profession, and no aspirations for one. Mother feared that Kathi and Stefan would end up living in poverty; or worse yet, Kathi would be the breadwinner of the household, a situation that was unacceptable in their culture.

There were plenty of other eligible bachelors in town. But Kathi loved Stefan, and she was going to marry him regardless of what anyone thought. Mother was deeply disturbed about this. It took her a long time to think it through. It was only when she remembered about her own wedding that she began to understand. Her father, Anna's grandfather, didn't want his daughter to marry a musician. Music was not a profession to him. Instead, he wanted her to marry a farmer or a bricklayer, but like Kathi, she had her mindset. Playing music alone would not generate enough income to support a family, so all the musicians in the Draxler Band had day jobs.

A wedding date on April 23, 1940, was set. Father Julius Morawetz from the Catholic Church would perform the ceremony. Father Morawetz announced the wedding at each Sunday mass for three weeks prior to the nuptials. As the date of the wedding got closer, Mother's disapproval subsided enough to start making preparations. She tailored a new dress for Anna. It was pale green with white lace around the collar.

On the day of the wedding, Kathi was at home, preparing her own dress. How beautiful she looked in her light-blue dress and flowers in her hair. A band played music as they walked behind the procession of family members led by Kathi arm in arm with her godparents. The music was provided by another local band because most of the Draxler Band musicians were at the wedding party.

They walked from the house to the courthouse where the wedding registration papers were signed by a magistrate. From there, it was on to the church where Stefan Latzkowitsch was already waiting along with his family. Father Morawetz performed the ritual, which was short and sweet. From the church, everyone walked two blocks to the Weber Music Hall for an afternoon of celebration.

There was plenty of food for all—draft beer and wine for the adults and flavored soda water or milk for the children. Once again, Anna was told to behave although Mother knew that was impossible for her. The party lasted well into the next day. The band played for many hours, even playing music while escorting guests to their homes. Kathi and Stefan moved in with Stefan's parents until they could afford their own place.

A learning opportunity

One day in late spring, Anna was walking home from school on lunch break when she decided to stop by the Weber General Store to look around. She enjoyed just looking at all the merchandise on the shelves. There was a man and woman standing inside the store by the front door, engaged in conversation. Anna looked down and saw some paper money on the floor. She walked over and picked it up.

She looked around to see if anyone had noticed her picking up the money. No one noticed, so she pocketed it and left the store. Anna continued her walk home. She passed another store that was closed for lunch. She walked around to the back door and knocked. The store owner answered the door and said, "What can I do for you, Anna?"

"I'd like to buy a pencil," Anna told him. She handed him the money she had found. Anna had never seen a hundred-dinar bill before, so she did not comprehend how much money she had found.

The store owner looked at Anna with a puzzled look. He went into the store and returned with a pencil and change for the bill. All that money in her hands was more than Anna had ever seen. It was more than she had room for in her pockets. She didn't know what to do with it.

She started feeling bad about what she had done. Instinctively, she knew it was wrong to walk out of the store without asking if anyone had lost the money. She hid the money in a crack between some bricks outside the shopkeeper's front gate and then ran home for lunch.

Anna went straight home after school. As she got closer to home, she could see a woman standing outside the front door, talking to Mother. She recognized the woman as the same one she saw in Weber's store earlier that day. Mother turned to Anna and asked, "Anna, is there anything you want to tell me? Do you have any money?"

"Yes, Mother. I found some on the floor at Weber's," Anna said. Mother said, "Give it all to me right now."

To which Anna replied, "I don't have it. I hid it." The woman standing next to Mother was becoming impatient and demanded her money. Mother told Anna to go get the money. Anna ran all the way to where she hid the money, hoping that it would still be there. She found the money, ran home, and handed it to Mother, which she promptly handed to the woman. Mother ordered Anna to go inside.

Anna knew she was in trouble and that there was going to be a lecture. Mother came in and, with tears in her eyes, told Anna to never, ever take anything that does not belong to her. Anna nodded in agreement and said, "Yes, Mother." She quickly forgave Anna.

Easter Sunday had arrived. The day before, Anna was busy collecting grass to make an Easter nest while Mother boiled eggs for coloring. Onion skins were used to make brown; flowers and beets were used for other colors. Anna loved this holiday because it involved eating eggs, candy, and a chocolate bunny.

Thursdays were market days. The church grounds provided space for townsfolk and people from neighboring towns to sell their goods in an open-air market. Garden produce, handmade clothing, pottery, flowers, baked goods, and live animals were sold. Anna loved looking at all these things.

The whole town was in bloom. The scent of the flowers from the acacia trees that lined the streets was intoxicating. Just about every house had fruit trees and a garden. The town was abuzz with people working the soil: planting, pulling weeds, and mending fences. Mother determined that her garden was not big enough to sustain the entire family, so she leased a patch of soil in another part of town to supplement. On occasion, Mother would literally drag Anna with her (she got to ride in the red wagon that Mother pulled) to the garden patch, about half a kilometer from their house. There, Anna was taught how to pull weeds, till the soil, and when the time was right, harvest vegetables. When rain levels were low, Mother would bring buckets of water for the plants. Meals at home were planned according to what vegetables were in season.

One afternoon, Mother said, "Come, Anna. We're going to pick chamomile flowers. Take this basket and come with me," Mother said to Anna. They both walked down to the banks of the Temesch River where the chamomile flowers were in full bloom. She taught Anna the correct way to pick the flowers. In no time at all, they filled the basket. Back at home, Mother spread a tablecloth on the lawn of the front yard and spread the chamomile flowers out to dry in the sun. When completely dry, the flowers would be gathered and put in a jar to make tea.

Summer

Summer was finally here, which meant school was out for summer vacation. Anna got her final report card. Her grades were average, except for sports where she excelled. Her brother Stefan always got straight As. The summers were hot and humid, with temperatures reaching into the nineties. Outside the front door and down at the end of the patio was a summer kitchen, complete with wood-burning stove and a table with bench seating. Most summer meals were cooked and consumed outside.

Anna remembered an incident that happened when she was five years old while at home alone. Mother had placed three one-gallon glass jars of cherries on a wooden bench in the backyard to ferment in the sun. Anna was playing in the yard when she saw a cat walking through the yard. She yelled at the cat, "Shoo, shoo!" But the cat was unfazed. Anna picked up a rock and threw it at the cat. That worked; the cat high-tailed out of the yard. Unfortunately for Anna, the rock she hurled at the cat ricocheted off a bigger rock in the yard and landed right on one of the glass jars of cherries, putting a crack in the glass.

Anna panicked, and without giving it much thought, she hid the broken jar in the garden behind some bushes, hoping Mother would not notice that one of the jars was missing. As soon as Mother got home, Anna asked if she could go over to Nani's house. She was hoping that when Mother found the broken jar, her anger would have subsided by the time Anna got home.

Before she even got to Nani's house, she heard Mother scream, "Anna, Anna!" She could tell by her tone that Mother was angry. "Why didn't you tell me about the jar? I followed the trail of red cherry juice to the bushes." Anna told Mother about the incident with the cat. Mother forgave Anna. She may have found Anna's story a bit amusing as Anna heard a faint chuckle from Mother as she walked away.

Introducing Little Anna

Kathi and her husband Stefan were still living with his parents. Mother forbade Anna to visit them. She was not given a reason why she was not allowed to see her own sister. Anna did not know Kathi was expecting a baby. Kathi and Stefan's baby girl was born on October 17, 1940. Her name was Anna, affectionately known as Little Anna. The news spread like wildfire through the town. Anna was an aunt at the age of seven!

One day, on her way home from school, Anna went to see Kathi against her Mother's orders. In honor of Mother's wishes, Kathi would not let her into the house, so she held up the baby to the window for Anna to look at. Anna had tears in her eyes as she gazed at this beautiful little baby. Years later, Mother told Anna why she was not allowed to visit Kathi. Mother never completely got over being angry at Kathi for marrying Stefan. Mother knew she was wrong and made up with Kathi after Stefan was killed in 1942, fighting in the German Army.

Fall

Autumn was harvesttime. Anna and her brother Stefan were tasked with helping Mother bring in the summer harvest. The temperature in late September was still quite warm and humid, which always made Anna miserable. Digging through the dirt with her hands to find potatoes was not her favorite pastime mostly because the dirt would get impacted under her fingernails.

The potatoes were put into burlap sacks for storage. Just before winter, Mother dug a large hole in the now-empty garden, placed straw on the floor of the hole, and put all the potatoes that were left on top of the straw. She then covered the potatoes with another layer of straw, dirt, and ashes. This prevented them from freezing in the winter. The potatoes could be retrieved as needed by digging a small hole and then covering it back up. Onions and garlic were braided and hung up in the storage room. Carrots and parsley roots were placed on the summer kitchen floor and covered with sand.

Sauerkraut

Sauerkraut was a staple in most German households. One day a year was designated as sauerkraut-making day. Harvested cabbage was brought into the kitchen, along with a large slicer. The cabbage heads were sliced and arranged in a big wooden barrel in the storage room. Layer by layer, the cabbage was salted and spiced with cara- way seeds and bay leaves until the barrel was full. The cabbage was pressed into the barrel and left to ferment, sometimes for weeks.

Mother had a reputation for making the best sauerkraut in town. Some of the gypsy women would come around and beg Mother for some sauerkraut. Mother had a kind heart and would never refuse anyone. She would tell Anna to keep an eye on the gypsy women while she went out to the storeroom to get the sauerkraut. The gypsies had a reputation for thievery, and Mother did not trust any of them.

November 1 was All Saints' Day. Most of the German families would go to church first, then walk to the cemetery to honor the dead. The only flowers in bloom at that time of year were chrysanthemums. To this day, the scent of these flowers reminds Anna of her home. In the evening, they lit candles for the loved one who had passed away.

Slaughtering of the pigs

December was the month when pigs were slaughtered. Walking to school on a December morning, Anna could hear pigs from other nearby houses screaming for their lives. Mother would have four or five pigs slaughtered in December.

Professional butchers were hired. Four men and three women would show up at their house early in the morning and set up tables in the backyard. They brought with them four or five huge butcher knives, sausage grinders, ropes, chains, a big wooden tub, and several large metal buckets. Two men entered the pigsty and caught one of the pigs. The pig was brought out of the sty and into the yard. The pig would kick, scream, and bite while being wrestled to the ground by one of the men.

Once pinned down, the second man would slit the pig's throat and catch the blood in a pan. The pig would bleed to death in about one minute. The big wooden tub was then filled with boiling water, and two chains were laid across the bottom of the tub and draped over the edges. The now-deceased pig was then submerged in the hot water, which made it easier to remove its hair from the skin with a scraper.

The two men would roll the pig over using the chains inside the tub. The pig was removed from the tub, and the scraping continued until the skin was clean. The pig was then hung by its hind legs from the wood beam overhanging at the edge of the patio roof. A wooden stick was used between the hind legs to keep them apart. When all the pigs were cleaned and hung in this manner, the process of butchering would commence. The metal buckets were placed under each pig to catch the remaining blood and internal organs.

Almost every bit of the pig would be used. The intestines were removed, cleaned, and used for sausage casing. All the meat and fat scraps left over from the butchering process were put through the meat grinder and made into sausage. The fat was boiled down to make lard. The meat was cut up into pieces suitable for smoking, but before that, it was packed in salt and stored in wooden barrels for several weeks.

The smoking of the meat took place in the house attic, which was referred to as the smokehouse. The meat was removed from the salt barrels and, along with the sausage, was hung from hooks on the wooden rafter in the attic. Metal pans were strategically placed on the attic floor to catch the dripping fat as the meat slowly dried out. The smoke from the kitchen oven was diverted from the chimney into the attic to bathe the hanging meat with smoke. The entire process of slaughtering four pigs took an entire day. A second day was needed to clean up the yard. Anna wanted so much to stay home from school for that first day. She thought she could be of some help, but really, she just wanted to watch. Mother believed Anna would just be in the way, so off to school she went.

Christmas

Christmas was quickly approaching. Anna would often stop at the open-air market next to the church on her way home from school. She wanted to see all the colorful Christmas decorations. There were gingerbread cookies cut out like Kristkindel (their version of Santa Clause), baked goods, candy canes, and beautiful dolls and toys—all handmade by the merchants themselves.

Anna remembers coming home from school while Mother was busy working in the kitchen. The whole house smelled like freshly baked cookies. "Oh, Mother, can I have a cookie?"

"Ja, nur ein" (only one), Mother said. Anna held it in her cupped hands, careful not to lose a crumb. "Schmekt gut?" (Taste good?) Mother would ask while nodding her head.

Anna remembers hiding under the kitchen table, sneaking bits of cookie dough while Mother was rolling out the dough and cutting shapes. Christmas was the happiest time of the year for Anna. The smell of baked goodies and the fragrance of Christmas trees were intoxicating to her. She remembers the sound of the fire crackling in the big oven while she and Stefan would play games.

Sometimes, Father would join in. He would get silly, and they would all laugh. That was a magical time for Anna. On Christmas Eve, they would all go to evening mass. Anna remembers being in church, with the organ playing and the town choir singing "Silent

Night." She felt such peace and joy, she could have listened to the choir all night. Father Morawetz brought in a figurine of the little baby Jesus and laid it on top of the straw in the little wooden manger of the Nativity scene set up inside the church.

Last Christmas with father

After mass, the family walked home arm in arm down Main Street. There was fresh snow on the ground, and Anna remembers the sound of the snow crunching under her feet with each step. Their walk home took them through the wealthier section of Setschan. They could see Christmas trees through the windows, all lit up with candles and tinsel. Anna says she still has this memory because it was the last Christmas she spent with her father.

Anna could hardly contain her excitement the closer she got to home. She anticipated that there would be a Christmas tree with gifts under it when they got home. Father unlocked the front door, and Anna pushed past him to be the first one in the house. To her disappointment, there was no Christmas tree and no gifts. Mother told her, "Kristkindel must be very busy. Just go to bed. Besides, she only comes while you are asleep." Anna went to bed.

Early the next morning, Anna woke to the smell of oranges and freshly baked cookies. On the table in the middle of the room was a one-meter-tall Christmas tree adorned with foil-wrapped walnuts and candy canes as ornaments. Under the tree was a bowl of oranges and cookies. Underneath the window in the front room was a little white cradle with beautiful flowered-printed bedding and a little rag doll in the middle. Anna couldn't remember a time when she was happier than that moment. Mother smiled at Anna and said, "You see? What did I tell you?" Christmas gifts were only given to chil- dren, so her parents did not receive any. Stefan got a set of dominoes. Mischi and Juri came home for Christmas dinner. Mother cooked her best meal of the year, a huge roasted goose with all the trimmings. After dinner, they had dessert, which was a type of stru- del. Anna spent the rest of the afternoon playing dominoes with Stefan and Father. Mischi and Juri sat around talking about work, playing music, and girls.

The Draxler Band took some time off from playing music to be with their families for Christmas. On New Year's Eve, the band started to play again. Father, Mischi, and Juri spent the day practicing, polishing their brass instruments and preparing their uniforms.

One year

This completes one year in the lives of the Friedrich family. They were a poor family, but they did not live in poverty. They had no television, not even a radio. They had no telephone, no running water, and the only source of heat was from the oven in the kitchen. They had electricity but only for a few hours a day; sometimes, none at all. The only form of transportation they used was their legs.

The townsfolk were surrounded by friends and family. Certainly, the Friedrich family loved each other although they did not show it openly. They were not overly affectionate. Everyone knew every- one, and they were kind and supportive of each other. Sure, there were squabbles and disagreements; that's human nature. The school encouraged the children to participate in sports and outdoor games. Families went to church together on Sundays. They loved all kinds of music and were always singing or whistling.

The townsfolk formed choirs and dance groups. They put on plays and showed films. The children were mostly well behaved. There was no violence, no drugs, no gangs, not even graffiti. Teens fell in love, got married, and started families of their own. Most of the men had trades or professions. Most of the women stayed home and took care of household matters. Some of the women helped in the fields. Everyone did their share; there were no slackers. Their lives were not easy, but they were happy. Little did the people of Setschan realize that their lives were about to change forever.

The coming of war

The year was 1941. Most of the townspeople of Setschan were oblivious to the war that was raging all around them. Some families owned a radio, so they were aware that there was a war going on in Europe. There was no sense of urgency about being sucked into the war, not until news was spread around town that German troops were headed their way.

April 6, 1941—Germany invaded Yugoslavia

Within ten days of the invasion, the Royal Yugoslav Army surrendered to the Nazis. On April 17, 1941, German soldiers marched into the town of Setschan. The soldiers were mostly Nazi SS. The SS officers remained in town for ten days. During that time, the Nazis called for all ethnic German men between the ages of eighteen and forty-five to join the German Army. At first, the ethnic German families were overjoyed to see the soldiers. For the first time in the history of Setschan, they were under German government control. For the past two hundred years, the region had been under Austrian, Turkish, Hungarian, or Serbian rule. The railroad, courthouse, post office, banks, and most government offices were under Serbian control.

The reality of war hit home when the first casualty occurred. While serving in the German Army, a Setschan resident named Peter Bohn was killed by Partisan Serbs. This affected the townspeople so much that they renamed the town Petersheim, Peter's Home.

Mischi in Berlin

Anna's oldest brother Mischi was a star pupil in school. Mischi's teacher, Johann Putz, saw tremendous potential in him to learn the architectural trade. Mr. Putz talked to Mother and Father about sending Mischi to an architectural school in Berlin, Germany. Father was all for the idea and even tried to talk Mother into moving to Berlin. Mother did not want to leave her home so that idea was quickly quelled. Father took out a bank loan against their house to pay the tuition for Mischi's training. Mischi had just turned eighteen years old, and luckily, he just missed being drafted into the German Army. In May 1941, Father and Mischi traveled to Berlin where Mischi was admitted into architectural school. Father remained in Berlin to work construction jobs.

In May 1941, Berlin was the epicenter of the Nazi campaign. At that time, the city was still intact and the fighting had not yet reached the city limits.

Home alone, summer 1941

With Father and Mischi in Berlin and Juri, then fifteen years old, working for a nearby farmer, Mother, Anna, and Stefan were left to do all the work around the house. To bring in a little extra money, Mother worked for a while that summer at a nearby farm that had a wheat-threshing machine. Anna was eight years old, and Stefan was ten when they were left alone for the first time in their lives.

Anna remembers one day in late summer, when two men showed up at their front door. One man was from the court, and the other from the bank. They demanded payment for the loan against the house that Father took out to pay for Mischi's tuition. Mother could not pay them any money, so they confiscated Mother's sewing machine.

As they were carrying it out the front door, Mother pleaded with them. She begged them not to take her sewing machine. That machine was everything to Mother. She used it almost every day, constantly mending and making new clothes. At one time, Anna wore underwear made up of four different scraps of cloth. Despite being laughed at by the other girls at school, Anna was proud of her underwear. Mother was heartbroken about losing her sewing machine.

Father and Mischi home again

In 1942, after being gone for an entire year, Father and Mischi came home. Soon after they returned, Mischi, nineteen; Juri, seventeen; and Stefan Latzkowitsch, twenty, joined the German Army. Father followed a short time later. Stefan Latzkowitsch was shot and killed shortly after he deployed. His battalion received almost no training and was considered expendable, as were most of the Schwaben German men who were sent to the front lines.

Mischi and Juri had a few things on their side. They were young and strong and, most of all, handsome. They were the epitome of the Aryan race. Mischi was sent to fight in the North African campaign under the command of Field Marshal Erwin Rommel, more commonly known as the Desert Fox. Anna was not sure where Juri was stationed. Mischi was captured by British forces and imprisoned in a British POW camp somewhere in Saharan Algeria. He rode out the rest of the war as a POW.

Mischi was eventually transferred to a POW camp in Egypt where he was released from in 1948. Because of his construction skills, Father was placed in charge of several reconstruction crews tasked with repairing damaged bridges. His superior officers allowed him to take leave and travel home for short periods.

The old bridge

The only bridge in Setschan was over the Temesch River at the east end of town. The old bridge was made of wood and was deteriorating. In the spring of 1942, the bridge was badly damaged by ice and rendered unusable. Since most of the men in Setschan were off fighting in the German Army, the only ones left to repair the bridge were old men and Serbians. In early summer of 1942, about thirty Serbian professional bridge builders living in neighboring towns were hired by the Serbian government to undertake the daunting task of replacing the wooden bridge with a steel one.

The project took almost two years to complete. The men working on the bridge stayed in Setschan during the workweek and went home on weekends. Mischi and Juri's bedroom was empty, so one of the Serbian men asked if he could rent the room in the Friedrich family's home. The man's name was Djurin.

Mother welcomed him, and soon, he was like part of the family. He ate meals with the family and slept in the brothers' bedroom. He worked on the bridge for ten hours a day during the week and traveled home on weekends to his hometown to be with his fiancée. During his lunch breaks, Djurin sometimes helped Anna carry the water bucket from the well four houses down the street from theirs. He would hold Anna's hand and whistle as they walked back to the house. Anna did not speak the Serb language very well, and he spoke very little German.

Djurin worked on the bridge until its completion in early 1944, when he returned to his home. The Friedrich family believed they would never see or hear from him again.

One Sunday in April 1944, Anna's class received their first holy communion. They had been practicing since January. Mother found a white dress and veil for Anna. Anna was sure Mother had borrowed the dress from someone else. Nevertheless, Anna was still proud to be wearing the dress. It was so beautiful and, for a short time, made her feel like an angel.

Caught between two giants

In September 1944, a caravan of horse-drawn wagons from Romania rolled through Setschan on their way to Germany. The wagons were loaded with supplies and personal belongings. The Romanians were spreading news around town that Russian troops were headed toward them. The Setschan townspeople were given the opportunity to evacuate with the Romanians. A few families that had relatives in Germany decided to escape the inevitable and joined the caravan.

Their intensions were to go back to Setschan one day and reclaim their property. Little did they realize that they could never go back. The rest of the townspeople chose to stay in their homes. To evacuate would be to give up everything they worked so hard for. The Friedrich family also stayed in their home. After all, Mother was eight months pregnant, and besides, they had no horses or a wagon.

Russian advance

Yugoslavia remained under German control from the time of the invasion in April 1941 until the failing German Reich was driven out of the country by the Yugoslavian Communist Partisans aided by the Russian Red Army in 1944.

One morning in early October 1944, as German soldiers were in retreat and were leaving Setschan, Nazi SS officers marched seven- teen Serbian men down to the Temesch River. The Nazis identified them as Communist Partisans. One of the SS officers systematically executed all the men and then dumped their bodies into shallow graves. The SS officers that committed these heinous acts departed Setschan along with the German soldiers in retreat. Their departure left the townsfolk to ostensibly bear the brunt of the responsibility for these murders. The ethnic Germans of Setschan feared that the families of the murdered Serbs would retaliate.

A group of Serbian Partisans from the nearby town of Neuzina, led by Arkadija Marcicew, a former butcher in Setschan, announced that for every Serb that was murdered by the Nazis, they would decapitate one hundred ethnic Germans from Setschan. To carry out this act of retribution, Marcicew needed permission from two offi- cials of the Serbian Communist Party. When permission from the court was denied, the group of Partisans disbanded.

There was a steady downpour of rain outside, fitting weather for what was about to happen. Kathi moved back home to care for her pregnant mother. The sound of gunshots and cannon fire were heard off in the distance but were steadily getting louder as the Russian troops got closer. Everyone was terrified. By midmorning, they could hear gunshots right outside their windows.

The Russian Red Army had entered Setschan, engaging German forces in fierce gun fighting. Many soldiers were killed from both sides. Kathi told everyone to sit under the kitchen table, out of the line of sight of any incoming stray bullets. Four-year-old Little Anna had no idea what was going on. She crawled under the table and sat next to eleven-year-old Anna. "What are we doing?" she asked.

Trying to hide her fear and not wanting to frighten Little Anna,

Anna told her, "We're playing a game." Anna looked over at her mother and saw her crying. She had only seen her mother cry like that once before when the men from the bank took away her sewing machine. Mother was Anna's rock. She was the strongest person Anna knew, the one person who was always in control of any situation. To see her crying uncontrollably only raised Anna's level of fear. Kathi tried to calm Mother down as she continued to cry and pray for their safety.

Anna imagined that any second, Russian soldiers would burst in through the front door with machine guns blazing, or worse, being impaled by their bayonets. By afternoon, the shooting had subsided. After a while, Kathi got up enough courage to walk to the side patio window where she could see down the street. She saw Russian soldiers running in all directions with rifles pointed straight ahead, ready to shoot at any enemy that crossed their paths. Anna and Stefan could not stand the suspense, so they crawled out from under the table to see what was going on outside. Kathi yelled at them to get back under the table.

The sounds of gunshots and explosions resumed and continued throughout the remainder of the day. No one dared step outside for fear of being shot. Kathi continued to look out the window, hoping to get a sense of what was happening. Kathi was now the strong one, trying to calm the rest of the family. Gradually, the sounds of gunfire became more distant and less frequent.

The Russian soldiers continued their advance through Setschan toward neighboring towns. Thankfully, none of the townspeople were injured or killed during the skirmish. By next morning, people emerged from their homes and hiding places. The fear of venturing outside lingered with many people. Kathi decided to go outside but just to the edge of the property. Anna and Stefan asked if they could go outside with Kathi. Mother replied sternly, "No, you stay inside."

They had been cooped up inside the house for almost two days now and were anxious to go outside. From the end of the front yard fence, Kathi could see all the way down the street. She saw the widow Frau Geiger who lived alone across the street, looking out her window. Eventually, more people went outside, and some of them gathered near the water well next to the Dengel home. Everyone seemed to be talking at the same time, asking questions and wanting to know what was going on.

They learned that the Russians took many horses, clothing, and food. "Has anyone heard any news on the radio?" Kathi heard one person ask. Later that afternoon, a messenger from the courthouse known as the Drummer stood on the street corner, beating on his drum until everyone came out of their homes and gathered around. The Drummer announced, "Everyone who owns a gun or radio must bring them to the courthouse immediately." He went on to say that no newspaper will be printed and no mail will be delivered. The school will be closed until further notice. The volume of chatter among the people rose dramatically as they were wondering what to do. This was the worst possible time to confiscate their radios. They felt they were being cut off from the rest of the world. The ethnic

Germans reluctantly turned in all the requested items.

After the Russians soldiers drove the Nazis out of Setschan, the Serbs saw it as their opportunity to move in and take control of the town. The Serbs took control of the courthouse, railroad station, and bank. They seized the bank accounts of all ethnic German families, rendering them penniless. Although she had nothing to forfeit, Kathi walked over to the courthouse to find out any news that she could. She then returned home to relay the news to Mother. "No mail," Mother cried out. "How are we going to know if your father or Mischi or Juri are alive?"

Kathi tried to comfort Mother. "Just think about your baby right now," she said.

Brother Karl

On October 16, 1944, with the help of a midwife, Mother gave birth to a healthy, strong baby boy. They named him Karl. Anna had tears of joy when she held this little baby boy in her arms for the first time.

Meanwhile, Serbs from the neighboring towns of Boca, Sartsch, and Neuzina took advantage of the frightened and vulnerable Schwaben German families. They rode into Setschan with wagons, mostly at night, to loot and plunder. They targeted the wealthy Swabian German families and took whatever they could get their hands on. Many of the wealthy households had Serbian maids, chauffeurs, apprentices, and farmhands working for them. They were trusted employees and knew where everything was located. Many of them turned against their employers and joined the pillaging: stealing jewelry, silverware, clothing, linens, smoked meats, wine, and brandy. With the men and boys fighting in the German Army, the only people left living in the town were women, children, and the elderly. The Swabian Germans were too frightened to fight back for fear of retaliation. Some of the Gypsies aided the Serbs by telling them where the valuable things were located. The looting and pillaging continued for what seemed like weeks, maybe months.

Much of the Yugoslavian population resented the eth- nic Germans. Not only the Serbs, but the Croats, Slovenian, and the Bosnians also hated the Germans. They hated that the ethnic Germans took over so much of their Yugoslavian territory. As the looting and terror in the region escalated, so did the Serbian disdain for the ethnic Germans. They considered them part of Nazi

Germany even though most of them had nothing to do with the war. Serb presence in Setschan grew almost daily. They moved into homes that were abandoned by Swabian German families fleeing to Germany. They drank up all the alcohol in town. They threw parties in the streets until all hours of the night, yelling and singing and fighting among themselves with total disregard for the other families living there.

On numerous occasions in late 1944, the Communist Partisan Serbs entered Setschan at night and, without any known reason, randomly targeted elderly German men by dragging them out of their beds and forcing them to walk barefoot for six kilometers to the nearby town of Neuzina. There they were beaten, tortured, or shot in the head. Many of the ethnic German men who were not killed died later from their injuries.

Some of the survivors were made to walk back to Setschan with almost no clothes on and barefoot, and then walk for another eighteen kilometers to the prison in Betschkerek. The prison building, called the Old Mill, was notorious for torturing and killing people in horrific ways. To satisfy their bloodlust, the Serbs cut off body parts from their victims and then laughed at them as they cried and begged for their lives. Very few people survived the Old Mill. Anna's grandfather, Jakob Rech, was one of the survivors, though he died later in the Rudolfsgnad concentration camp.

Swabian German men from Setschan were disappearing almost every night. They slept in their clothes and shoes for fear that they would be next.

German families hid what valuables they had left in wooden boxes and buried them in their backyards or inside their barns. Along with any money or jewelry were family photos; musical instruments; uniforms; and survival items such as canned fruits, jams, and smoked meats. Those items were carefully wrapped with cloth and placed into the boxes. Mother buried their box inside the barn and covered the spot with straw.

Transport to Russia

On December 26, 1944, the Drummer from the courthouse came out and made an announcement: Any German men left in Setschan between ages seventeen and forty-five and all German women age seventeen to thirty-five were ordered to show up at the courthouse at eight o'clock the following morning. They were advised to pack clothing and food enough for two weeks. They were told by the communist soldiers that they would travel to neighboring towns to search the harvested cornfields for any residual corn left by the farmers.

Dr. Todt, the Hungarian town doctor, was tasked with weeding out the weak, sick, and women with children with no one to care for them while they were gone. Those people were excused from this work detail and were allowed to return home. Kathi was one of the women sent home because Dr. Todt gave testimony that Kathi had a heart condition and that she was not fit for this type of work.

Some 115 mostly women with a few men from Setschan were chosen. These men and women were forced to walk to Modosch, a nearby town, twelve kilometers away and right on the Romanian border. When they arrived there, they were met by other groups of selected men and women from neighboring towns. Everyone's belongings were loaded onto a wagon. The people were forced onto train cattle cars and locked in from the outside. They were locked in the cattle cars for seventeen days without provisions: no running water, no heat, and no toilets. The only food they had was what they could carry in their pockets. The soldiers gave them a small amount of water every day.

The train did not move during those seventeen days due to Romanian border closure. When the border finally opened, the train proceeded through Romania and on to Russia. When they arrived in Russia, they were put into labor camps, similar to the infamous Russian Gulag. The conditions were even more horrible than the cattle cars. They were given a five-year sentence of hard labor, just because they were ethnic German. The 115 people from Setschan were forced to work as slave labor for the Russian government. Most of them did not survive.

The leader of the band died

In March 1945, Anna's Opa Jacob Friedrich, died. He had been very sick for months before he finally succumbed to pneumonia. He was sixty-nine years old. A week before he died, Mother, Anna, Stefan, and five-month-old Karl went to visit him. Opa's bed was in the far-left corner of the front room. Anna remembers sitting in a chair next to his bed in front of an open window. She remembers thinking what a beautiful spring day it was. Karl was speaking baby talk as he sat on Anna's lap, his arms flailing about in no particular pattern. Opa's eyes glazed over with tears of happiness as he watched Karl. "He reminds me so much of your father when he was a baby," Opa said.

Jakob Friedrich was a physically big man with a commanding presence. He led the Draxler Band with a whip and kindness mixed together. His off-time profession was repairing clocks and watches. This was evident by the number of clocks in all stages of disrepair all around the house.

Mother and Oma walked over to his bedside and pulled the down-filled comforter and sheet off Opa to expose his legs. Anna saw that his legs were swollen and bluish green in color. Oma began to cry. She said that Dr. Todt had been checking on him and said there was nothing more he could do for him. There was no medication available that he could administer that would help alleviate his pain. Opa died a few days later.

The ghetto

On March 25, 1945, Frau Geiger from across the street was shouting from her window. "Kathi, hurry! The soldiers are driving everyone out of their homes." Mother was washing the breakfast dishes when they heard Frau Geiger. Anna got up from the floor in the front room where she had been playing with five-month-old Karl. She ran to the window to see what all the commotion was about. Mother picked up Karl from the floor and ran outside to the patio fence. From there, she saw several townspeople going door to door to announce the warning.

Frau Geiger ran across the street to talk to Mother. She told Mother, "Gather your money, valuables and some food, and put them into bundles." She went on to tell Mother to put on as many clothes as she and her children can wear.

Mother did not hesitate as she jumped into action. She ran back into the house and called, "Anna, Stefan! Put on as many clothes as you can." Mother was calm but firm. "Anna, gather up the baby's things and wrap them up in your green scarf. Hurry!"

"Why, Mother, what's going on?" Anna asked. Mother explained that the soldiers were locking people out of their homes. Anna was confused and didn't know what that meant. She knew by the tone of Mother's voice that this was serious and she must obey immediately. Mother and Stefan ran out to the hidden box they buried beneath the barn floor to get more supplies. Mother then ran to the storage room next to the summer kitchen and gathered what little food was left. The soldiers took most of their food weeks earlier. Mother had hidden some smoked ham, bacon, and smoked sausage. She grabbed as much as she could carry, wrapped it all in towels, and said to Stefan, "You finish here while I go check on Anna." Stefan reburied the box, smoothed the dirt over it with his hands, and covered the spot with straw.

Anna put on a thick flannel dress, one that Mother had made for her out of a blanket. Over that dress, she slipped on another warm dress. She then pulled a sweater, with difficulty, over her head. She gathered diapers, clothes, and blankets for Karl while Mother wrapped what little money she had in a handkerchief and shoved it into her bra. Stefan was busy filling a basket with as much food and towels as he could carry. He and Anna put on their heavy winter coats and shoes. Anna could hardly move. She had so much clothing on. They could tell by the sound of the shouting outside that the soldiers were getting closer.

Anna looked out the front room window and saw her neighbors being herded down the middle of the street by soldiers pointing rifles at them. Ten minutes had passed. They were all trembling with fear. Just as Anna bent down to pick up Karl, the soldiers burst into the front door with rifles pointing at them and screaming, "Raus, raus!" (Out, out). One of the soldiers went through every room in the house to make sure no one was hiding. Another soldier stood at the front door, and Anna had to pass right by him to go outside. She hesitated and looked at Mother. "Go ahead, Anna," Mother told her. Anna stepped sideways past the soldier to go outside, being careful not to get too close to him. She held on to Karl as tightly as she could. She could hear her dog, Daxi, barking in the backyard; but she could not go to him. "It's okay, Daxi. I'm coming back!" she shouted to the dog over the fence. Stefan and Mother followed with their bundles and baskets. Mother was the last one out the door when the soldier at the door held out his hand and demanded the front door key. Mother hesitated, then handed him the key. There were more soldiers outside pointing to the street and yelling at them in Serbian to walk. They all walked down the middle of the street toward Main Street. They met up with other people walking in the same direction. So many people were walking down the middle of the street at one time. Anna asked everyone she met, "Where are we going? Do you know what is going on?"

Anna struggled to keep up with Mother and Stefan. Karl was happy, not aware of what was happening. He was playing with Anna's face and talking baby talk. Anna could hear questions being asked all around her. "Why are we being thrown out of our homes? Do you know what will happen to us?" people were asking. Many of them just walked in stunned silence. Some of the neighborhood dogs jumped the fence and were barking at the soldiers. Mostly, they were ignored, but if any dog became a threat to the soldiers, the dog was shot. There were potholes in the streets, and Anna prayed that she would not fall with Karl. An old woman just ahead of her fell, but Anna could not help her. She held on to Karl as if her life depended on it. She had so many clothes on she couldn't feel him next to her. Mother looked over at Anna and saw that she was struggling. She slowed down to let Anna catch up.

They walked for about forty minutes. The soldiers were every-where, blocking the side streets and forcing all of them into one sec-tion of town at the west end of Setschan. One of the higher-ranking soldiers announced that everyone will need to find quarters wherever they could. The announcement created chaos and confusion as the townspeople walked around in a daze with no idea what was hap-pening. Some of the people had relatives living in that part of town that they could stay with. Others were forced into any home that had room, sometimes twenty-five to thirty people to a home. Anna's Oma Rech lived in that section of town. She was alone since Opa, Jacob Rech, was abducted by communist Serbs and sent to the Old Mill. She welcomed the Friedrich family into her home. Kathi and Little Anna joined them there. She had a small house, just one bedroom and a kitchen.

All the townspeople were weak with fear. Oma Rech couldn't stop crying. Mother was exhausted and collapsed onto the kitchen floor. Kathi went around checking on family members and reassuring them that everything would be all right, that they had to be strong and wait this out.

No one was allowed to cross to the other side of town or try to go home. Communist Serb soldiers patrolled the perimeter of this newly formed ghetto. Everyone was worried about who would feed their animals. Anna was thinking about Daxi and wondered who would care for him. Days turned into weeks. People were overcome with feelings of despair and hopelessness. "When can they go home?" they asked the soldiers. No one gave them an answer.

Daxi

It had been over three weeks and still no word about when they would be allowed to go home. Anna was sitting outside in front of Oma's house when she heard a familiar bark. She looked up to see Daxi running toward her. She was so glad to see him. Anna picked him up and ran into the house. "Mother, Mother, look! He found us! What a smart dog you are," Anna repeated.

Mother looked at Anna with sadness and said, "You must send him home, Anna. You know he can't stay here."

Anna replied with tears in her eyes, "But Mother." Anna wanted to argue, but she knew Mother was right. Anna took Daxi outside. "I'll get you a drink of water," she told the dog. She went over to the water well and cupped her hands to hold some water. When she returned with the handful of water, she saw several boys teasing Daxi, poking him with sticks. "Stop that!" Anna cried out. "That's my dog!"

One of the boys replied, "Oh ja, what are you going to do with him? You can't keep him here. There isn't enough food to feed him."

Anna knew she had to send Daxi home. She pet his head and told him to go home, but he just stood there and looked at her with his tail wagging. "Go home," Anna said sternly. Daxi's expression turned to sadness as he slowly turned toward home. One of the boys threw a rock at him, causing him to run. Anna cried for an hour over her dog.

Home again

At the end of the third week, soldiers were walking down the street shouting, "Everyone go home." People were so happy that many began running home. "Take the food that you brought. You will need it," Oma said.

"Thank you, Mother," Anna's mother said. They looked at each other for a while with love and sadness in their eyes.

Everyone breathed sighs of relief, thinking the worst is over. They were excited to go home, but they were also apprehensive about what they might find there. Most of the furniture had been removed by the soldiers. As soon as they got home, Anna announced that she wanted to see Daxi. She ran to the backyard where Daxi was kept, and she called out his name. "Daxi, Daxi," but there was no response. It took a few minutes, but Daxi finally came around. He slowly moved toward Anna, his head hanging down, emaciated and barely able to walk. His whole body shook, and there was fear in his eyes.

When Mother saw him, she shook her head and with sadness in her eyes and said, "Come on, Anna. We have work to do inside. Stefan will take care of Daxi." Mother looked at Stefan as if to tell him without words what she needed him to do.

They went inside and started cleaning house when Stefan walked in from outside and said, "I can't do it."

"But you have to," Mother told him. "I don't want him to suffer." Stefan turned around and walked back outside. Anna followed him outside and called out, "Daxi, Daxi." Suddenly, Anna realized what was going on. "No, no!" she screamed. Mother came outside and put her arm around Anna as if to hold her back. She watched as Daxi followed Stefan around to the far side of the barn.

Mother told Anna, "I'm sorry, Anna. He is sick, and it would be cruel to make him suffer. You stay here until Stefan comes back." Anna knew in her heart that it was the best thing to do. She loved that dog so much. When Stefan returned without Daxi, she knew he was gone. She ran into the barn and cried for hours. Mother left Anna to grieve for a while until she finally went out to the barn to talk to Anna. "I know you loved that dog, and you were very brave to let him go. So many bad things have happened to us that we must stay together to survive. We must be strong." Anna nodded her head in agreement.

Ghetto again

Tension was beginning to subside a bit. All their farm animals were commandeered by the soldiers. That didn't stop Mother from planting and tending to the garden. Anna was wondering if she was ever going back to school again. It had been seven months since she last attended school. They were into the second week of being back home when, at eight in the morning, they heard shouting in the streets again.

This time, the soldiers came much quicker and the people had little time to gather their things before being forced out onto the street. Anna put on as many clothes as she could. Again, Mother stashed her money into her bra. Anna gathered Karl's things. Mother collected as much food as she could. "Ach du lieber Gott!" (Oh my dear god!) Mother was saying repeatedly. In the confusion and chaos, Mother forgot to close the storage box hidden in the barn. Once again, the communist soldiers burst in the front door with rifles in hand, shouting, "Raus, raus, mach schnell!" (Out, out, quickly!) Again, families were being herded like cattle. Only this time, they were taken to the front of the courthouse. There were many more soldiers, and they seemed to be more organized than last time. The people were ordered to form lines and wait to go inside the court-house, one at a time.

Kathi and Little Anna joined Mother, Anna and Stefan already in line. People were confused and crying. Anna watched one woman take off her wedding ring and swallow it. "I'm not letting them take my wedding ring," she said in defiance.

The soldiers were shouting, "Schnell, schnell!" pushing people to move faster. Anna noticed that people were going into the court-house, but no one came out. *What are they doing in there?* she thought to herself. They stood in line for hours. As they moved closer to the entrance of the courthouse, Anna looked at Mother and asked her what was going to happen to her inside.

Mother put her arm around Anna while holding Karl in her

other arm. "Don't be afraid, Anna. They're not going to hurt you." She smiled at Anna and gave her a reassuring nod.

There were four entrance doors, and people were shoved into all of them, one at a time. Anna was having a difficult time hiding her fear. One of the doors opened, and the soldier standing next to it ordered Anna to go inside. Again, Mother said to Anna, "Go ahead, Anna. It's okay."

She walked through the huge entryway and into the first room. There, she saw an older man with gray hair and a thick mustache in a distinguished-looking uniform, sitting behind a wooden desk. Standing next to him was a regular soldier with a machine gun in his hands. Anna looked around the room and saw boxes lined up against the wall, overflowing with clothes, jewelry, toys, shoes, and bundles of smoked meats.

The man behind the desk asked Anna in German with a deep voice, "How old are you?"

"Eleven," Anna answered. He turned to the soldier and said something in Serbian. He then turned his attention back to Anna, "Take off your earrings." Anna stood there, trembling with fear as she removed her earrings. "How many dresses are you wearing?" He made a gesture to the soldier to lift Anna's outer dress to see. Anna thought to herself, *Oh god, please don't make me take my dresses off.* He told her to take off one dress. "You don't need two dresses," he said. He ordered her to put the dress and her coat into one of the boxes. He then gestured to her to go outside and wait. The soldier pushed Anna through a different door that led to the backyard. He pointed to a group of young girls Anna's age.

Outside, Anna saw several large groups of girls, boys, and adults huddled together, many of them crying. "They took every-thing," one woman cried as she walked by Anna. Two of Anna's school friends, Leni and Maria, smiled when they saw Anna walk toward them. "We're so glad to see you, Anna," said one of the girls. "You were always the brave one." Anna's attention was focused on the courthouse doors, watching and waiting for Mother and Kathi to come out. Mother finally came out the door and immediately walked toward a group of women holding infants. Anna walked over to Mother and was surprised to see her still holding a bundle. "They took all of Karl's clothes and left me with a few diapers."

Everyone was getting hungry and thirsty, especially the children. No one knew when or even if they would get any food from their captors. Anna thought, *Thank God Karl is being nursed by Mother.* Kathi and Little Anna came out the door and were put into a differ- ent group from Mother. Stefan joined a group of boys his age. The yard was getting crowded.

The soldiers started taking groups to assigned houses. Mother's group went first. Kathi's group of mothers with young children went next. Anna had no idea where the soldiers were taking them. Anna's group of adolescent and teen girls was taken to Adam Weber's home, right across the street from the courthouse.

Anna's new home

Anna was part of a group of about eighty young girls. They all entered the house through the side door and into the kitchen. The house was very large. All the rooms were empty. All the furniture had been commandeered by the soldiers. The house had three large bedrooms, a maid's quarter, a huge living room, and an enormous kitchen, where most of the meals were eaten. Outside was a covered patio with a picnic table and bench seating. The property had its own water well and an outhouse in the backyard.

The girls were running through the halls, in and out of the bedrooms, laughing and screaming, totally oblivious to the nightmare they were about to enter into. Three adult women walked into the house: Frau Keller, Frau Schneider, and third woman Anna couldn't remember. "Okay, girls," Frau Keller announced sternly. "Listen very carefully. All of you find a spot where you will sleep every night."

The girls looked around, shrugging their shoulders and looking at each other in puzzlement until one of the girls spoke out, "Where are we going to sleep? There are no beds."

"You're going to sleep on the floor on top of straw that you will need to bring in yourselves," said one of the women.

"We are all hungry and thirsty. Are we going to get anything to eat?" one of the other girls asked.

Then all the other girls said in unison, "Ja, I am hungry too." "There is no food. Now hurry up and make your beds," Frau Schneider told them. The girls went outside and walked over to the barn one by one to bring an armful of straw into the house.

There were no blankets or pillows. There was also no electricity and no heat even though there was a fireplace in the living room. When everyone had settled down and things got quieter, Anna could hear girls crying. She started thinking about her family, wondering where they were and if she would ever see them again. She began to weep silently. Anna was exhausted and fell asleep on top of her pile of straw.

Anna woke up the next morning to the sun shining and birds chirping. Some of the girls were already up and gone, looking for their loved ones. She untied her braids to make it easier to pick the straw from her hair. She wandered into the kitchen where she was greeted by Frau Keller. "Go sit outside at the picnic table. Here's some hot soup." The soup was made from browned flour mixed with water and a little salt. Anna sat with some other girls who were eating their soup. After finishing the soup, Anna asked Frau Keller if she knew where her mother and sister were taken. "Your mother is at the Reinhardt's house, and Kathi is at the Lenhardt house," the Frau said.

"Danke," Anna said to her and left.

Soldiers were everywhere, patrolling the streets with rifles and machine guns in their hands. The townspeople were not allowed to leave the heavily guarded area but were allowed to walk around the ghetto itself. Anna found her mother and Karl and hugged them both. She was overjoyed to see them even though it had been only one day since she last saw them. She wondered where her two omas were. Anna's brother Stefan was in a nearby house with other boys close to his age.

Anna's cousin, Juri Rech, was working as a horse handler for the soldiers. He saw Stefan one day and asked him to come and work with him. "I don't know anything about horses," Stefan said.

"You just watch me. You can learn. I will teach you," Juri said. Stefan agreed, and the soldiers allowed him to join Juri in the horse barn. He started out by cleaning horse stalls, shoveling manure, and spreading straw on the floor. The two boys did not live in the ghetto with the other boys. Instead, they slept in the stables with the horses. At age fourteen, Stefan was quickly promoted to carriage driver for some of the military officers.

A couple of weeks went by when one of the barbers from Setschan, Leopold Lenhardt, nicknamed Boldi, was ordered by the soldiers to cut off all the girls' and women's hair. He just didn't know how he was going to break the news to them. He went to his mother first and told her he was ordered to cut everyone's hair off. The women became hysterical when they heard. Some started crying loudly; some were screaming. Boldi's mother, not wanting her son to get hurt, stepped up and said, "Cut my hair off first. They can't hurt me by cutting my hair off! Cut it off," she said in a defiant tone.

The example she set echoed around the ghetto. Pretty soon, all the females in the ghetto had their hair cut. The women put on scarves, but Anna's group of girls did not. There were gypsies and Serbs just outside the ghetto, making fun of the girls and laughing at them from across the street. They called them "plucked chickens." The girls wore their short haircuts as a badge of courage.

By June 1945, the stench from the overused outhouse in the backyard of the Weber house permeated the entire area. The women put lime down the toilet hole to keep the smell down, but they quickly ran out of lime and the outhouse use multiplied by ten. The water was not drinkable as people were coming down with dysentery. By that time, all the people were infested with head lice and fleas.

All children over the age of ten were required to work. Anna was eleven and a half. Most of the boys worked in the fields, collecting as much vegetables and fruits as they could find all around their own deserted homes. All the food they found went to feeding the soldiers. The girls were required to show up at the courthouse every morning for work detail. They were assigned tasks like hunting for eggs or grain or whatever food they could find. The girls were heavily guarded and monitored to stop them from stealing food. Some of the

women were sent to cook and do laundry for the soldiers.

One morning, Anna was ordered to work in the field. Soldiers drove all the girls chosen for this task out to the fields in a horse-drawn wagon. The soldiers stopped, and the girls were ordered off the wagon. One of the soldiers looked at Anna and pointed to a plow on the ground. He motioned her to unharness the horse from the wagon and strap it in to pull the plow.

Anna had never been near a horse before. She had never plowed a field either. One of the Serb farmhands came over to the wagon to help Anna unlatch the horse and then walked it over to the plow. He showed Anna how to strap in the horse, and then disappeared. Anna got the horse strapped in and the plow pointed in the right direction. She had only watched this being done from a distance at neighboring farms.

She positioned herself behind the plow, grabbed the reigns, and snapped them to signal the horse to start pulling. Luckily for Anna, the horse knew what to do. The plow began to move. She had a hard time holding on because the handles were too high for her. The plow began to veer off track, and the horse was going too fast for Anna to keep up. When the plow reached the end of the field, she didn't know how to stop the horse.

She remembered watching the farmers. When they came back from the field, they would pull back on the reigns and shout, "Whoa, whoa!" She tried that technique, and it worked. The horse slowed down to a full stop. She then walked out in front of the horse, grabbed the harness, and pulled it around until the horse faced the opposite direction. She felt very lucky that it was a gentle horse that went along with whatever she commanded of it. *Thank God*, she thought. She only had to do that for two days.

Some of the younger women with small children, like Anna's sister Kathi, were sent to work with the soldiers in their warehouses. The communist soldiers converted several houses into storage warehouses, where they stockpiled all the townsfolk's confiscated personal belongings. In one house, they stored clothing; in another, it was bedding. Kathi's job was to sort all the items. They separated the furniture; alcohol; canned food; and smoked meat such as ham, bacon, and sausage. After a few weeks, the meat started to go rancid. It was all put into a huge pile with no air circulation.

Some of the women on this work detail would take small items such as combs, clothing, and soap—items they could stuff into their pockets. The soldiers would turn the other way and pretend not see what workers were doing. The owners of the houses that were converted into warehouses had secret ways to get in and out of them. They revealed these secrets to some of the women. These women would sneak out at night and run, very covertly, to the warehouses. They used the secret window or door to gain entry. Once inside, they had their pick of whatever clothes and food items they could carry. For a while, the women and girls had a little extra food until one of the women informed the soldiers. The women were caught and punished, and that was the end of the extra food. The punishment doled out by the soldiers was brutal and often included rape.

One day, while standing in line for her next work assignment, Anna saw a Serb mother and her four-year-old girl walking across the street from the ghetto. The little girl was clutching a rag doll in her arm. Anna thought the doll looked familiar. "Hey, that's my doll," she said to herself out loud. Anna remembered that Mother made that doll for her. She loved that doll and was heartbroken to see another girl holding it. She watched the little girl a while and could tell she loved that doll as much as Anna did. Eventually, she felt okay about letting the little rag doll go.

Home run

Anna did get a few days when she did not have to work. She spent those days with Mother or Kathi. Anna remembered one of those days. It was a warm day in June 1945 when Karl was taking a nap, and Mother was washing clothes. Anna was sitting outside on a bench, just daydreaming and taking in the sunshine. She was thinking how badly she wanted to be at home again. She had thought many times about running home. She had heard of others that had run home to retrieve hidden items on their property. Anna did not tell anyone about her plan. She watched the soldier for a while and learned their patterns. Most of the time, the soldiers were standing around, smoking cigarettes. Anna planned her route. She knew every house from the ghetto to home. She only had to cross two streets. The soldiers were patrolling the streets, so it was risky.

That night, Anna was so excited, she could hardly sleep. She was going over her plan in her head. The next morning, she went to visit Mother and saw that she was busy with Karl. She went outside and stood in front of the house. Her heart began to race as she watched the soldiers patrolling up and down the street. As soon as they turned around toward the Temesch River, she dashed across the street to the corner house, jumped over the fence, and hid in the garden. She waited there for a minute to catch her breath.

As soon as she thought it was safe, she jumped over the fences from garden to garden until she reached the next street. There were no more animals left in the pens making noises, so she had to be very quiet. She looked both ways up and down the street. She saw no one, so she ran across the street and jumped the fence into the garden of the home at the end of her block. Just three more fences, and she'd be home. Finally, she was in her own backyard. She was surprised at how different everything looked. The weeds were as tall as she was.

She remembered the smells of the fruit trees and flowers. Even the weeds smelled better than the air in the ghetto. She wanted so much to go inside the house. She walked up to the front door, and to her surprise, it was unlocked. She walked into the house and looked in every room. The house was completely empty. The door to the oven in the kitchen was left open. She looked inside it and saw a small box of family photos, slightly burned on the edges. Anna was just about to pick up the photos when she heard men's voices coming from the street.

She quickly ran into the backyard and lay down on her belly in the middle of the tall weeds. She could hear the men walk up and down the patio, checking the door and windows. One of the men opened the gate into the backyard. Anna froze and held her hand over her mouth for fear of being heard breathing. The wind was blowing the weeds back and forth. She could see the soldiers' boots as they stood there in silence, looking out over the yard full of weeds. Finally, one of the soldiers said something in Serbian to the other, and they both left the property.

Anna stayed there for another half an hour until she worked up the courage to get up and run back to the ghetto the same way she came, dodging all the patrolling soldiers. By the time she got to the Reinhardt house where Mother was staying, she was out of breath and her face was flushed. "What's wrong, Anna? Why are you out of breath?" Mother asked. She had no clue what Anna had just done.

Anna visited Mother every evening after her evening meal. One warm June night in 1945, Mother anxiously said to Anna, "I don't know why the sore behind Karl's ear won't heal. Anna was holding him while Mother applied an herbal mixture to the sore. It didn't seem to bother Karl. He was as happy as ever, always laughing and smiling. Mother said she would take him to Dr. Todt tomorrow.

The next morning, Mother took Karl to see the doctor. He told her, "I'm very sorry, I have no medicine to give him. Keep it clean and keep applying the herbs." Mother took him back to the ghetto, and later that evening, she cried.

Herr Dengel

In early July 1945, the soldiers selected five girls for a work assignment. Leni, Kathi, Nani, Maria, and Anna were selected for the job. They were each given a basket and told to go out to the abandoned homes and hunt for eggs and whatever other food they could find. A soldier with a rifle went with them to make sure they didn't stray from their assignment. When they approached Anna's house, she got excited and said to herself, "Oh boy, we're going to my house." Instead, the soldier motioned for them to cross the street and go to Frau Geiger's house. Kathi and Anna went to the garden to look for vegetables. The other three girls went to the chicken coop to look for eggs.

Anna's mind began to wander, and soon, she was daydreaming. Kathi went over to her and tried to snap her out of it. Suddenly, Kathi, Anna, and the soldier heard a loud scream coming from the chicken coop. "There's a man sleeping in the chicken coop," one of the girls screamed. The soldier ran toward the coop with his rifle pointed straight ahead, ready to attack.

The soldier encountered the old man in the coop and began yelling at him in Serbian, "Out, get out! Up, up," all the while pointing the barrel of his rifle at the old man. Anna's jaw dropped when she saw who the old man was. "It's Herr Dengel," she whispered to herself. *What was he doing there, dressed in ragged clothes?* she thought. Herr Dengel worked on the railroad with the Serbs and Hungarians. He lived in the corner house next to the water pump and was neighbors with Frau Geiger. Herr Dengel was dragged out of bed by the communist soldiers and taken to the Old Mill in Betschkerek about eight months ago. He was a sickly man with failing health. After surviving being beaten and tortured by the soldiers, he was transferred to a hospital in Kathreinsfeld, about twenty kilometers

from Betschkerek.

While in the hospital, he escaped and came back to Setschan. When the soldiers started driving everyone out of their homes, the only place he could find to hide was the chicken coop.

The soldier forced him to walk at gunpoint toward the ghetto. The girls were ordered to follow. When they got back to the ghetto, the soldier put Herr Dengel in a jail cell at the courthouse.

It was evening when the five girls from the work detail got back to their quarters. Anna walked in and immediately heard some of the girls complaining, "Beans, beans, beans, that's all we ever get are beans. I'm sick of them."

Frau Keller barked at them, "Quit complaining. Be happy you have something to eat."

"I love beans. Can I have your share?" Anna asked. "Sure, Anna. Go ahead. It's yours."

An example

One evening in July 1945, Anna was sitting outside on a bench with Mother and Karl when they suddenly heard screaming and yelling coming from the street. They all got up and ran to the fence to see what was going on. They saw people being forced by soldiers with rifles to walk to the Temesch River.

Before they could even turn around, the soldiers came crashing into Mother's quarters, ordering everyone out onto the street. They, too, were told to walk to the Temesch River with everyone else. Everyone was terrified. They remembered when the seventeen Serbian men were forced by Nazi soldiers to walk down to the river bank where they were executed. No one knew what was going on or what was going to happen to them. Many of them believed that this was retribution for the deaths of those seventeen Serbian men.

Anna held on to Mother's dress. She did not want to be separated from her. When they got to the Temesch, the soldiers lined everyone up at the top of the levee with their backs to the river bank.

There were over three hundred ethnic German people standing in a long line. They all thought they were going to be shot and dumped into the ravine next to the levee. Five soldiers with rifles pointing straight ahead walked up to the line of people. As the soldiers got closer, Anna and Mother could see that the soldiers were escorting someone.

Mother gasped when she realized who it was. "Oh my god, it's Herr Dengel," said Mother. His hands were tied behind his back as he was being led to the bottom of the ravine. The soldiers demanded that his family come to the front of the crowd. His wife, Elizabeth, their four young children, and his mother came forward. One of the soldiers announced, "I wanted all of you to see what happens if you try to escape or run away." Herr Dengel had tears in his eyes as he looked at his family. His mother and children were also crying.

The soldier looked at the family members as he ordered the other four soldiers to fire their weapons at Herr Dengel. His body fell to the ground as blood was spurting from his head and chest. Herr Dengel's mother collapsed to the ground in horror. Elizabeth held back her tears, not wanting the soldiers to see her cry. Some of the people in the crowd started to sob; others stood frozen with fear and shock. The crowd was told to go back to their quarters. Most of the people walked back slowly with heads down.

"How could this happen?" Anna heard someone say. As they were walking back, Anna saw her cousin Juri drive by in a horse-drawn wagon, headed in the direction of the execution site. Anna thought for a second, *What the heck is he doing?* Juri had no idea what just happened at the river. He was going to the riverbank to collect cloverleafs.

The Reinhardt house was the first one they came to. Anna and Mother sat down in silence on the same wooden bench. Anna slowly arose from her state of shock. "Mother, I have a confession to make." Anna told her about the events of the afternoon when they came upon Herr Dengel in Frau Geiger's chicken coop. "Oh, Mother, it's our fault. We should have left him alone." Anna felt a deep sense of sorrow and guilt as her mother tried to console her.

"Anna, you have to try to forget what you saw today. It's not your fault." Then Mother said in a stern voice, "You must forget. Do you understand me? Forget what you saw!" Karl started to cry, and Mother turned her attention to him. Her demeanor changed to a sweet, loving mother as she cuddled her son. Anna spent most of that night crying. No matter what Mother told her, she still felt responsible for Herr Dengel's execution.

Juri and another man were coming back from their cloverleaf run when a soldier stepped out onto the road in front of Juri's wagon and held out his hand in a motion to stop, shouting "Stoj!" (Stop!) The soldier ordered the two men to take their wagon back to the river. When Juri arrived there, he saw several soldiers standing next to a ravine. He looked into the ravine and saw what looked like a dead person covered with blood and lying face down in the mud. One of the soldiers hollered out to Juri, "Take the corpse to the ass cemetery, animal cemetery, and bury him there. If you tell anyone where his body is buried, you will be executed."

Juri and the other man lifted the body out of the ravine and onto his wagon. They quickly covered the body with cloverleafs and drove their wagon toward the animal cemetery. As soon as the soldiers were out of sight, Juri stopped the wagon and said to the other man, "Let's dig a hole right here and put the body in it. We can cover it with branches and leaves and mark the location with this stone. That way, we can find it when we come back later when things settle down. I will tell the family where the body is, and they can retrieve him and bury him in the people's cemetery."

Typhus outbreak

A few weeks after the incident with Herr Dengel, Anna's cous- ins Juri, sixteen, and his ten-year-old sister Nani were diagnosed with typhus. Juri survived the fever but never got the chance to tell the Dengel family where he buried their father.

One evening when Anna was visiting, she saw her mother crying. "I don't have any more herbs. I've used them all up." Another woman sitting nearby overheard Mother and came over to tell her where to find a certain herb growing in town.

"You won't find any growing here in the ghetto," she told Mother.

Mother turned to Anna said, "I need you to sneak out of the ghetto and go to Wolf Klosi's house." Mother drew a picture of the herb onto Anna's palm with the burnt end of a piece of twig and said, "Bring the leaves and the roots."

"Okay, Mother. I will," Anna said. Mother gave Anna an apron to wrap the herbs in. Again, Anna's heart began to race. She thought about the two soldiers in the backyard the first time she ran home. She was nervous but pushed passed it and got herself ready. She knew the way. She headed out the same way as before. Only this time, she had to make a right turn when she reached the second street. The Klosis's house was the second from the corner. She ran over to the house, and just like Mother described, the plant was there on the property. She pulled up as many of the plants as she could, roots and all, and rolled them up in the apron. When she returned, Mother breathed a sigh of relief. She pulverized the plants into a paste consistency with a stone and immediately applied some to Karl's infection.

Most of the women Kathi's age were assigned to work in the fields. Kathi's heart condition made it dangerous for her to do any hard labor. Instead, Kathi was assigned to care for about ten small children, ages three to five. Some of the women working in the field became resentful of Kathi not doing her share of the hard work. They complained so much that Kathi agreed to take someone's place in the field. That day, there was a huge storm passing through the area with heavy rain and hail. Kathi was drenched and soon got very sick.

Kathi was taken to the Fendt house hospital where she was diagnosed with typhus.

Two houses, the Merschdorf house and the Fendt house, were converted into makeshift hospitals. Both houses were next to each other and across the street from the ghetto.

Condition got worse

Typhus and dysentery broke out all over the ghetto. They experienced an infestation of flees, lice, and rats throughout the ghetto, which aided in the spread of typhus. They had no way to combat these pests, so the infestations continued to get worse.

A shipment of typhus vaccine was finally sent to the ghetto. Everyone who didn't already have typhus was inoculated; those who did have it were not. Kathi was already diagnosed with typhus, so she did not get the vaccination. Many people contracted typhus, and many of them did not survive. Anna did not remember if she had the fever.

Karl's condition got worse. The sore behind his ear had now become a hole. Mother was overcome with fear and desperation. She and Anna took Karl back to Dr. Todt, and the doctor said, "I have no medicine to give him. The only thing I can do is cauterize the sore."

The doctor had no anesthetic to give Karl. He pressed a red-hot kitchen knife against Karl's sore spot. Karl screamed like they never heard before *What a horrible thing to do to a baby*, Anna thought. Karl's condition continued to get worse. His thyroid gland swelled, and he couldn't swallow. He began to have trouble breathing and became very weak.

Mother held Karl in her arms, trying to comfort him. She put him in his little makeshift crib. In the middle of the night, Mother was awoken by the sound of Karl banging his arms against the sides of the crib. Mother jumped up from the floor where she was sleeping and ran over to Karl. He looked like he was gasping for air. Mother panicked and started screaming, "Help me! Somebody help me, please!"

Some of the other mothers got up and helped Mother take the crib outside. "He needs fresh air!" Mother yelled. They got the crib outside, and Mother stood next to it, helplessly watching her son choke for air until he stopped struggling and his body went limp. One of the other women ran to get Dr. Todt. He just told her that Karl had *krebs* (cancer), and there was nothing he could do for the boy.

Karl died

Early the next morning, Mother walked over to Anna's quarters at the Weber house. All the windows were open; there were no screens. Some of the girls were sitting on the windowsills and talking. Mother asked one of the girls if she knew Anna Friedrich. "Ja, she is still sleeping."

"Could you tell her that her little brother died?" Mother said.

Anna heard what Mother had told the girls, and she jumped

up and ran outside and into Mother's arms. They both cried as they held each other. Mother said, "Dr. Todt should have told me about Karl's condition. I would never have let him cauterize Karl's wound. It was too much pain to put him through." Anna and Mother went inside and looked at Karl. He looked so peaceful. There were some other women sitting around Karl and praying. Karl Friedrich died on August 11, 1945. He was ten months old.

Onkel Nick Friedrich, Father's oldest brother, lived in another town about ninety kilometers from Setschan. He somehow eluded the soldiers when they came through his town. He hid in his own home, keeping out of sight of the soldiers. When he heard about Karl's death, he came to Setschan immediately.

Mother was not allowed to go to the cemetery. Only certain people were assigned to remove bodies from the ghetto. Some relatives from the Rech side of the family made arrangements. They had German friends with Hungarian last names who were spared the ghetto. They got permission for Mother to bury her son in the cemetery. Anna's Grandmother Rech owned a mausoleum at the cemetery, and she allowed Karl to be buried there. Mother had no coffin, so she bundled Karl's body in a bedsheet. Anna and Mother carried Karl to the cemetery. Onkel Nick was there and had opened the tomb. Inside the tomb were three coffins containing two adults and one child. Onkel Nick opened one of the adult coffins and placed Karl's body in on top of the corpse that was already in it. They all said a prayer for Karl and then left. Onkel Nick stayed to close everything up again.

After Karl was gone, Mother spent every waking minute caring for Kathi and helping some of the other patients in the hospital. Anna went back to her quarter. The other girls there left her alone, mostly because they just didn't know what to say to her. Anna was not allowed in the hospital. All she could do was wait and pray that her sister and mother emerge from the hospital all well. What Anna didn't know yet was that Mother came down with typhus fever as well while in the hospital caring for Kathi.

Goats

One day, Anna was selected along with three other girls for the task of tending to a herd of goats. Their job consisted of going over to the empty house where the goats were corralled at night, let them out of their pen, and herd them over to a nearby meadow to feed on the grasses there. They used sticks to keep the goats moving in a straight line. There were six female goats and one male. The male goat was left tied up at the house. He was far too aggressive and protective of his harem to be turned loose. They untied him when they got back with the female goats.

An old woman came every evening to milk the goats. One day, while herding the goats toward the meadow, Anna stopped and noticed that there was no one to be seen in any direction. The weary soldiers knew the girls could not run, so they didn't follow them and keep an eye on them even though they were ordered to do so. Anna thought about how good some of that goats' milk would taste.

The next morning before the goat routine commenced, Anna looked around the empty house for a container of some kind. She found a dirty coffee cup and wiped it out with the hem of her dress. That morning while herding the goats to the meadow, Anna stopped and looked in every direction. When she saw that the soldiers were no longer in sight, she told the other girls about her plan to drink some goat milk. Anna gave each girl their assignment. One girl kept lookout, another girl held the goat steady, one girl did the milking—that was Anna's part—and the last girl held the cup.

The plan was successful. Each girl got one cup of milk to drink.

The girls continued this process every day for the next three days until one evening when the milk lady came and noticed that the goats were putting out much less milk than usual. The soldiers in charge of the goat milk brigade were scratching their heads, trying to figure out why this was happening. Anna decided it would be wise to stop for a while before they figured out where the milk was going. Anna smiled a bit to herself for having gotten away with something.

More family died

In the morning of September 9, 1945, Frau Schneider found Anna and told her that her cousin Nani Rech died the night before. Anna just sat in her little space, all alone, and cried for hours. That afternoon, Nani was taken to the cemetery to the same tomb where Karl was placed. Onkel Nick was there once again and, as before, had everything ready. Nani was laid to rest inside the other adult coffin on top of its occupant. Nani's mother, Oma Friedrich, and Oma Rech were also there at the tomb site. They said a prayer and left. Like before, Onkel Nick took care of everything. Nani Rech died on September 8, 1945. She was ten years old.

Three days after they buried Nani, Oma Rech came to the Weber house looking for Anna. She was crying while she put her arms around Anna. She softly and slowly told Anna that her sister Kathi died. "Oh god, oh no. Not Kathi, please no!" Anna collapsed onto the floor and bawled louder than she ever had before. Oma Rech tried to comfort her. "She had overcome the typhus, but her heart was too weak," Oma told her. "She died of heart failure."

Katherina Friedrich Latzkowitsch died on September 11, 1945. She was twenty-four years old. She was the mother of Little Anna, age five, and wife to Stefan Latzkowitsch, who was killed in 1943 while fighting in the German Army. He was twenty-five years old when he died.

Oma Rech and Anna went to the Fendt hospital and demanded to see Kathi's body. She was lying outside on the patio on a cot. "Where is Mother?" Anna asked. Oma Rech told Anna that her mother was also sick with typhus fever. Anna broke down and cried loudly. She said she wanted to see her mother. "You can't see her right now. You might catch the fever yourself," Oma Rech said.

Mother was unaware of Kathi's death. The nurses at the hospital didn't know how to tell Frau Friedrich that her daughter had died. A little while later, they helped her sit up and then told her. Mother was too sick to react. She lay back down, closed her eyes, and began to weep.

Kathi's body was taken to the Rech tomb for burial. Once again, Onkel Nick was waiting there for them at the cemetery. Like before, he had everything opened up and ready. The two adult caskets were full. Onkel Nick took Karl's body out, laid Kathi inside that casket, and then laid Karl back in on top of her legs. Onkel Nick stayed to close everything back up.

Lisle (Elisabeth) took care of Little Anna while Kathi was in the hospital. As soon as Anna returned from the cemetery, she went to visit Little Anna. Anna held her in her arms when Little Anna asked where her mother was. Up until that moment, telling her five-year-old niece that her mother was never coming back was the hardest thing she had ever done. They both held each other tight and cried for a long time.

Anna's job of tending to the goats every day continued. One evening, while finishing the day's work, she heard the girls calling, "Anna, Anna, come here, quick! One of the goats climbed the ladder inside the barn up to the attic. You need to get it down before the soldiers come, or we will all get in trouble."

"Why did you leave the gate open?" Anna scolded. The girls just looked at her without answering. Anna climbed up the ladder and crawled through the trapdoor into the attic. "I don't see any goats up here." She walked over to the edge of the attic and scolded the girls for playing a trick on her. Just then, she heard the trapdoor slam shut and the male goat was standing on top of the door. He put his head down as if getting ready to charge. Anna ducked behind a wooden post and began to pray. She said, "O God, please help me out of this mess."

The girls were trying to push the door open from below, but the goat standing on the door made it too heavy to move. Anna remained quiet, thinking about how she would get away. The goat finally forgot about her and walked to the other side of the attic. The girls pushed the trapdoor open, and Anna made her escape. "We still have to get the goat down," the girls said.

"Well then, someone will need to go up with me and try to force him down the ladder," Anna told them. Maria agreed to help Anna, so they both climbed the ladder to the attic. Both girls got behind the goat and pushed him by the rump forcing him down the ladder. Anna found an old bottle in the attic, brought it down, and filled it with goat's milk. She took the bottle of milk to the hospital to give to her mother. Anna found an open window and climbed up to the ledge. With one hand holding onto the window ledge and the other holding the bottle, she called out, "Please give this to my mother. It will make her feel better." Anna walked back to her quarters at the Weber house. She was thinking that life couldn't get much worse. That thought would soon be proven wrong.

Anna's mother, Katarina, 80, 1984

Anna's kindergarten picture, bottom row, first on left
In Setschan 1938, age 5

Draxler Band, top row, 4th from left, Mischko Friedrich.
Second row, first on left, Klosi Friedrich, both Anna's Uncles.
In the middle, Jakob Friedrich, band leader.
Bottom row, middle, Anna's father Stefan,
next on right, Anna's brother, Mischi, 1932

Slaughtering of the Pigs, (1938)

Typical street with church centrally located in the village of Setschan

Anna's first communion,
April 23, 1944, in Setschan,
Age - 10

Anna's brother Mischi Friedrich,
In the German Army, 1942

Anna's sister Kathi, with her husband, Stefan Latzkowitch,
and child, Annemarie, in Setschan, 1941

Kathi, Annemarie, Anna, (age 9), and Stefan, in Setschan, 1943

STEVEN G. KAUTNER

Anna's Friedrich Grandparents
Jakob and Elizabeth, with children
from left: Mischko, Klosi, Stefan
(Anna's Father), and Katharina
in Setschan around 1915

Anna's Rech Grandparents
Peter and Elizabeth, with children
from left: Katharina (Anna's Mother)
Georg, and Hans, in Setschan
around 1920

From left: Anna, Mother, Stefan, and Annamarie
In Vienna, Austria, 1950

Anna's siblings, from left:

Mischi – age 4

Juri – age 2

Kathi – age 6

Anna's siblings, from left:

Juri, Kathi, Mischi, Anna (age 5)

and Stefan in Setschan about 1938.

Juri   Anna   Stefan   Mishi

Anna and her brothers, 1984

Anna's adult children, from left; Steven, Helga, Rosemarie, Anne, and Eric, 2000.

Leaving Setschan

In the early morning of September 27, 1945, two communist soldiers stormed into the Weber house and started yelling, "Auf, auf, mach schnell," (Get up, get up, quick), at the same time banging on the doors with their rifle butts. The girls were startled by this rude awakening. Anna became frightened and jumped up. Half in a daze, she wondered why the soldiers were doing this.

"Did we oversleep?" Frau Keller was running around frantically, not knowing what to do. She tried talking Serbian to one of the soldiers, but he just pushed her aside. All the girls stood there in complete confusion.

One of the girls said, "Where do we have to work today that we were awoken so early?"

Because they all slept in their clothes and shoes, it did not take long to get ready. Anna shook her head to get the straw out of her newly grown short hair and then brushed it off her dress. Lisle and Nani, not Anna's cousin Nani that died, started to cry. *Why is it always the same girls that start to cry and then the others join in? Why do they always have to cry?* Anna asked herself rhetorically. She turned to Maria and said, "I'm not going to let the soldiers see me crying." Anna was one of the first girls out of the house. She walked to the fence along Main Street where she saw people coming from every direction of the ghetto. Armed soldiers were everywhere. "Where did all these soldiers come from? I've never seen so many soldiers," Anna whispered to herself.

The soldiers were herding the crowd of people down the street with rifles in their hands. They pushed the people to make them walk faster, yelling, "Schnell!" Some elderly people that could not move very fast were repeatedly yelled at by the soldiers. Everyone was confused about what was going on. Anna wondered what all these people were doing on the street. She thought, *They can't all be going to work this early in the morning.*

She heard someone in the crowd yelling, "They're shipping us out of Setschan!"

Anna's thoughts immediately turned to her mother. *Oh my god, what am I going to do? She's sick and can't walk. I can't leave here with- out her. I must go back to find her. I can't leave her,* Anna thought.

Anna started running through the crowd toward the hospital. She hoped none of the soldiers would notice her running in a different direction than the rest of the people. She counted the houses as she ran. No one paid any attention to her. She made it to the Fendt house hospital where Mother was. She walked across the patio and into the house through the kitchen. A woman with a towel wrapped around her nose and mouth tending to the sick yelled at Anna, "You shouldn't be here, Anna. You will get sick too." Anna ignored her and continued looking for her mother.

She ran into the front room, and there her mother was, lying on the floor on top of some straw along with about eight more sick people. Anna went over and knelt next to her. She whispered, "Mother, Mother." She did not respond. Again, Anna said, "Mother, Mother, are you awake?" Anna started shaking her by the shoulder, desperate to get a response. She started to cry, "Please, Mother. Please talk to me."

Mother finally opened her eyes. She lifted her head a little and looked at Anna. Anna cried even louder. She wanted to hug Mother, but she knew she shouldn't. After they looked at each other for a minute, Mother said, "Wer bist du?" (Who are you?)

"I'm Anna, your daughter." Mother looked puzzled as she tried to figure out who this young girl was in front of her. She lay her head back down and closed her eyes. Anna cried and prayed, "O God, please don't take my mother too. I need her. I can't lose another family member." Mother looked pale and emaciated. Her lips were cracked and white.

A soldier stormed into the room with his rifle in his hands. He must have seen Anna running through the crowd and followed her. He struck the butt of his rifle against the door and ordered Anna to get out. "Geh raus!" he shouted. Anna kissed her mother on the forehead, stood up, wiped the tears from her face with her dress sleeve, brushed the hair from her face with her fingers, and walked to the door. She stopped and turned around to look at her mother one more time. With the soldier behind her, shoving the barrel of his rifle into Anna's back and shouting, "Schnell," she walked out of the house.

Anna ran back into the crowd. She wondered if she would ever see her mother again. She felt helplessly alone and lost. Tears rolled down her cheeks as she walked in silence with her head down. Anna quickly snapped out of her feelings of hopelessness and started looking for anyone left of her family and friends. She wondered where Little Anna was, hoping that she was with Kathi's friend, Lisle. The soldiers were herding all the people toward the train station.

When they reached the train station, the people were crammed together, standing next to the tracks and waiting for the next train. Anna squeezed her way to the front of the station where there was an iron railing. She stepped onto the railing to get up higher than the crowd. She searched desperately for anyone she recognized. The noise from the people and soldiers was deafening. Anna heard children screaming, adults crying, people calling out loudly for their loved ones, people complaining, and others praying out loud. She saw frightened faces. Some looked like they were in shock; others appeared almost comatose with fear.

Anna saw Frau Keller and asked her, "Have you seen Friedrich or Rech Omas?"

"Nein," she said. "I cannot find my own family."

Anna pushed her way to the edge of the station platform and looked up and down the tracks. "How long do we have to wait for the train?" she asked out loud. "Does anyone know where the train is going to?" After waiting several hours, the train finally pulled up to the station on track number three. This was not a passenger train but a very long cattle train with only cattle cars. Anna was thinking, *This does not look good.*

Hundreds of soldiers surrounded the crowd and started yelling, "Everyone, move to the train!" Some of the soldiers started opening the doors to the cattle cars.

The crowd began to cry even louder than ever. "Oh my god, they're taking us to Russia to be used as slave labor!" someone screamed. Everyone was horrified as they were being pushed from behind by the rifle barrels of the soldiers toward the cattle cars. The soldiers told everyone to climb into the cars. Older people and children fell as they crossed the train tracks. People were in shock or were too stunned to help them. Sick people that could not climb the step up into the cars were pulled up by people already loaded into the cars. The soldiers packed as many people as they could into each cattle car.

Anna hoisted herself up into the car. By the time the soldiers were done, there was standing room only in each cattle car. The people did manage to sit down, some on top of each other. They waited for hours until the soldiers closed the doors to the train cars and locked them from the outside. That was when the real panic set in. People were screaming and crying, their arms flailing about and banging on the walls of the cattle car. Some couldn't hold their bowels due to immense fear. There were no toilets in the train cars, so the smell of excrement, urine, and vomit permeated the air. People were screaming out to the soldiers, "Please, we cannot breathe. Please open the door!" The cattle cars only had two small rectangular windows with steel bars over the opening meant to circulate air only while the train was moving.

Anna thought about all the family members that she lost. She had not heard a word from Father, Mischi, and Juri. She didn't even know if they were still alive. She hadn't heard from Stefan for months. She thought about her mother and felt a pain in her heart she'd never experienced before.

Suddenly, the train whistle blew, and the train lurched forward. Slowly at first, then building speed. Anna heard people crying, "They took everything we had, even our animals."

"They killed some of our husbands too," someone else said. "We worked so hard for them, and this is what we get." "Where is God now, where is he?" someone demanded to know.

Anna was exhausted and fell asleep on the floor next to a kindly old woman she did not recognize. Anna was awoken by the feeling of the train slowing down. The people started screaming and banging with their fists against the wall of the car. The train started to move again. This pattern of stopping and going went on well into the night.

Years later, the *Setschaner Rundbrief* (*Setschan News*) magazine reported that 750 people from Setschan were transported to Molidorf and Rudolfsgnad concentration camp. Every time the train stopped, it picked up more prisoners from different towns. By the time it got to the final stop, the number was estimated to be over 1,200. They had been crammed into those cattle cars for over twelve hours. The train arrived in the city of Betschkerek. All the doors to the cars were opened. One of the soldiers started yelling, another translating into German. "Sick and old people out first, and someone to walk with them." Eventually, everyone got off the train. Anna was cold and tired. She just followed everyone else.

All 1,200 people were transferred to another train, one that was used for hauling wood or coal. It was a cold night; and all Anna wore was the heavy dress Mother made for her, underwear, and shoes. She climbed up into the coal car, sat on the cold metal floor, pulled her knees up to her chin, pulled her dress over her legs, crossed her arms on top of her knees, lay her head on her arms, and went to sleep.

She woke from her sleep when the train stopped hours later. The train car doors opened; and soldiers were yelling, pointing to some wagons. "Raus, raus, everybody out! Mothers with small children over there." Anna heard horses snorting. She looked around to see where the sounds were coming from. She saw a line of horse-drawn wagons with a civilian driver on each one. "Old people and the sick in those wagons." The rest of them were told to line up and start walking.

It was the middle of a very cold night. Everyone was tired and shivering. Anna tried to walk between adults, hoping it would keep her warmer. She heard one woman say, "There was a sign back at the train station that said we were in Zerne."

Anna asked the woman next to her, "What are we doing in

Zerne?" What kind of work are we going to do here?"

Someone in the crowd said, "Just keep on walking. You will see when we get there."

Just then, Anna heard someone calling, "Anna, wo bist du, where are you?" Anna looked around and saw the kindly old woman she met when they first got on the train back in Setschan. The woman worked her way through the crowd to get closer to Anna, "Here, take my hand," she said. She had a soft voice like Mother, which gave Anna comfort. Anna remembered there was a full moon. She was cold, hungry, thirsty, and her legs were starting to give out. Her shoes, already too small, were hurting her feet.

Molidorf concentration camp

They walked for hours until they came to a small town called Molidorf located inside the Banat region, about 150 kilometers north of Belgrade, Serbia. The town had once been home to about one thousand Schwaben Germans. The soldiers announced to the people that they had reached their final destination and that they would start giving out housing assignments. The people started looking around. "It's just like our town of Setschan," someone said.

The houses looked similar, and so did the streets. The town was also deserted, just like Setschan. All the houses in Molidorf were completely empty. There was no livestock left in the barns, no animals in the yards. There might have been an occasional chicken or domestic cat running around loose. It was a beautiful autumn day. The sun was out, and the leaves were whirling all around. What the incoming detainees felt and saw was so surreal that they may have thought they were in a dream.

On September 28, 1945, the soldiers started separating people into groups. Like before, the mothers with babies were in one house and young girls in another house. The elderly were housed with their own families. This process went on until all 1,200 people, were assigned to a house with up to twenty-five people per house.

Each house had an outhouse in the backyard. Like Setschan, several water well hand pumps were positioned around town. Once inside their assigned houses, everyone was somber and just too exhausted to do anything more. Most of them just slumped to the floor where they stood and fell asleep. It was so overcrowded that no one could walk one meter without stepping on someone else. Anna had never experienced such hunger in her life. All she could think about was when she would eat again.

Anna was assigned to a corner house. The floor plan was just like her house in Setschan. All the housing for the Swabian Germans living in the Banat region of Yugoslavia were built around the same time by the same construction contractor and were designed by architects from Vienna, Austria. Only wealthy people who were will- ing to pay a premium were allowed to deviate from the government housing plans. Many of the houses in that region were over one hundred years old.

Anna was part of a group of fourteen young girls. They stayed close to each other as they explored the new environment they were forced to live in. The front door, which was actually right in the middle of one side of the house, opened into the kitchen. To each side of the kitchen was one room. To the right, facing the street, was the front room. Anna and her group of girls were the first to look in the front room. It was empty except for some straw on a wooden floor. "I guess we are going to sleep in here," Anna said. To the left side of the kitchen was a smaller combination bedroom and food storage area. Empty shelves lined one wall. The girls ventured outside in the yard and the barn. One of the girls found some old pots and pans in the barn, next to the stairway to the attic.

Later that morning, a woman named Frau Anna Friedrich, along with her daughter, Kathi, came into Anna's house and announced that she would be taking care of all the girls assigned to that house. Her daughter was ten years old. Though they shared the same last name, they were no relation to Anna. With the addition of Kathi, Anna's group grew to fifteen girls.

They soon learned that Frau Friedrich was not only kind, but she would do anything in her power to defend and protect the girls. They did not yet know what horrible things could happen to young girls when undisciplined soldiers were around.

The front door leading into the kitchen had six glass squares. Anna's room was about ten square meters and had a brick structure in one corner. The structure, measuring about three feet by three-and-a-half feet by five feet high, was the back side of the oven in the kitchen. It had a small door that when left open would allow heat from the oven to pass into the front room. The main door to the oven opened into the kitchen. The front room had three windows, two windows facing the street and one facing the front yard and patio.

Hunger was unremitting. The girls asked Frau Friedrich when they would get some food. "I do not know yet where or when we will get food," she said. With that, the frau left and returned a short time later and announced the good news. "They are setting up a food kitchen down the street in the fourth house to the right, and we will need to go there to get food. Driven by extreme hunger, the girls immediately started running down the street looking for the kitchen. Frau Friedrich ran outside after them and yelled at them to come back inside. "The kitchen is not fully set up yet, so it might be a while yet before we get fed," she told them.

One of the girls said, "Oh my god, we are so hungry right now. What do we do?" With great disappointment, the girls walked back to their house, threw themselves on the floor, and began to cry. One of the girls asked, "What are we going to carry the food in? We have nothing to put the food in to bring it back here." Anna remembered the old pots and pans found earlier by one of the girls, hidden in the outside pantry. Anna and Maria ran outside to find them. Anna found a pot that held about two liters. There were some smaller pots but nothing bigger. Anna started to salivate, thinking about *eintopt* (potato) goulash with sauerkraut, sausage, and bread.

Frau Friedrich gave the girls tasks to take their mind off their bellies. "Go outside and bring in enough straw to cover the floor of the front room." It seemed like at night when they went to sleep, all the straw was piled up underneath them, and when they awoke the next morning, it was in the middle of room and they were lying on the bare floor. The frau told some of the other girls to go outside and find some bricks and boards and bring them inside.

Some of the girls complained, "We are tired and weak from hunger. We cannot work!"

"Do what I tell you and quit complaining," the frau told them. Reluctantly, the girls slowly walked outside and looked around. They found what they needed in and around the barn. Frau Friedrich showed them how to line up the bricks on the floor and prop the wooden boards up against them to form barriers to hold in the straw. Each person had their own space. Wooden boards were placed on top of the bricks to form sitting benches.

Ten more women moved into the back room to the left of the kitchen. Frau Mueller was one of the women, along with her three-year-old daughter, Evi, who had blond hair and brown eyes.

The first few days in the camp, before they were forced by soldiers to work, there was nothing to do. They lay around the house thinking about the food they had at home. The trains kept bringing in more prisoners. Through the front room window, they watched a steady stream of people walking in the street, looking for a room or anywhere they could find space in one of the houses. The camp was already overcrowded. It's been several days since they last had any food.

Anna was glad to have her little piece of the floor. She slept in her beige flannel dress; she had no coat or sweater as those were confiscated by the soldiers back at the courthouse in Setschan. Anna heard one of the girls cry out for her mother. It made Anna think about her own mother, wondering if she was still alive and if she would ever see her again.

When Anna awoke the following morning, she noticed that several of the girls were already up and gone. They ran straight to the food kitchen. Anna ran out the door and toward the kitchen when she saw the girls slowly walking back to the house. She could tell by the looks on their faces that there still was no food. Anna had to see for herself, so she ran over to where the kitchen was set up. She saw eight huge steel kettles but saw no smoke coming from the kettle pipes. She heard a woman yelling, "Nein weir haben kein holtz" (We have no wood).

When Anna got back to the house, Frau Friedrich was waiting for everyone to return. She said, "Listen to me now. We can cry and complain, or we can do something about it. I want you to go up into the attic in the barn. Get down on your knees and look on the floor for any corn kernels, seeds, grain—anything you can find that we can eat." When they got up into the attic, it was dark and took a few minutes for their eyes to adjust to the dim light. To their delight, the floor was covered with corn kernels and wheat grain. The girls got down on their hands and knees and collected as much as they could carry in their rolled-up dresses. All the other girls were overjoyed when they saw how much they had collected.

Everyone's eyes were on Frau Friedrich as she prepared to cook the corn and wheat in the two-liter pot they found earlier. Frau Friedrich then said, "We need to go outside and find some wood for a fire." Anna spoke out, "I know where there is some wood. It's stacked up against the barn wall." The girls ran to the barn again and brought all the wood they could find back into the house. They stored some of the wood in the front room behind the brick oven.

It took a while for the stove to get hot enough to cook. The girls all stood around the kitchen, anxiously watching Frau Friedrich. The smell of the cooked corn was driving all of them crazy. It had been three days since any of them had eaten. As Frau Friedrich prepared to dole out the cooked corn, the girls, in a starvation frenzy, rushed the frau and circled around her to be the first to get fed. One spoonful for each girl, placed in their hands, was all they got.

Roll call

Starting on the third day in the Molidorf concentration camp, the soldiers began roll call at five in the morning. The camp commandant, Lieutenant Colonel Danilov Kesic, occasionally made surprise appearances at roll call to spout out orders.

Kesic moved into a house just down the street from where Anna was residing. He had a reputation as a mean, hateful, sadistic man that loved torturing people to the point of laughing as he tortured old men and young women, many of them his own countrymen. One of his legs was shorter than the other, which caused him to limp. That morning, about 150 young German women and old men were ordered to walk ten kilometers along with a squad of armed soldiers to the town of Zerne, where they were put to work in a makeshift warehouse, sorting and separating household and personal items the soldiers took from the German homes in Molidorf and other nearby German towns. The same thing happened in Setschan while the ethnic German people were in the ghetto.

The soldiers watched the prisoners carefully to make sure they didn't steal anything. Those that did try to steal something and were caught were severely beaten by one or more soldiers. In the evening, after working a fourteen-hour day, they were forced to walk back to camp carrying twenty-five kilo burlap sacks full of cornmeal and dried peas. The women were desperate for food to give to their chil- dren. They would make a small hole in the sack and catch what- ever came out and put it in their pockets. Some of the women were caught and severely beaten. After working for fourteen hours of hard labor and then another four hours of walking to and from Molidorf, they were given little to no food all day.

Every day was a workday regardless of the weather. The people were so weak from hunger they could barely walk. On rainy days, the roads became muddy, and with the loads they were forced to carry, their feet would sink deep into the mud. Their shoes would get stuck in the mud, and with the soldiers pushing them to march faster, they were forced to abandon their shoes and walk the rest of the way barefoot.

The next day, Anna woke up early, hoping to be one of the first in line for the food kitchen. When she got there, she saw a very long line already waiting. Anna waited in the food line for several hours. When it was finally her turn, she held out her pot with both hands. The woman serving the food scooped up one ladle of soup and poured it into the pot. Anna looked into her pot and saw water mixed with a little cornmeal, no salt and no fat, just water. She drank the soup down as fast as she could, hoping to get back into line for seconds. "No seconds today," they were told by the woman behind the kettles.

The little bit of soup they had did little to quell their hunger. Anna thought that if she had to stand in line for so long, she might as well get into the line for her next meal right then. When they finally did get food, it was the same soup but with a little extra, plus a one-inch square of corn bread. The extra in the soup were about fifteen dried peas and some black bits they couldn't quite identify except that the bits had legs. They fished out the bugs with their fingers and drank down the soup. The bread was made from cornmeal and water, with no salt and no fat, baked just long enough to hold together.

After a few weeks, they didn't even fish out the bugs anymore but instead just drank it all down, occasionally getting a bug stuck between their teeth. Anna remembered the crunch the bugs made as she chewed on them. There were rainy days when they got no food at all because they ran out of firewood or the wood was too wet to burn. Anna roamed through the streets, behind the houses, looking for anything edible. She found a few horseradish roots in the ground in one of the gardens. She wiped off the dirt from the roots and gobbled them down.

Frau Friedrich knew that many of the young women and girls were being raped and beaten by the soldiers. The frau did what she could to protect the girls in her house. Anna was oblivious to the abuse and torture, at least until the frau warned them to stay away from the soldiers and not to give them any reason to separate anyone from the rest of the girls.

When the weather was warm, Frau Friedrich encouraged the girls to go outside and get some sun and fresh air. Despite the constant hunger that gnawed at their stomachs, the girls kept themselves busy by playing games, and for a short while, they would forget about their hunger.

November was the start of rainy season. The girls would get drenched waiting in line for food. They shivered with cold as they waited for their clothes to dry. When it rained very hard, they stayed indoors and skipped meals to avoid getting wet again.

There was no running water, no showers, soap, towels, or toothbrushes. They had one small comb that they all shared. There were no sheets, blankets, or pillows. They found some old rags in the barn that the farmers once used to cover their horses during the cold of winter. The girls brought the rugs inside and used them as blankets or bedding.

As autumn progressed, the temperatures got colder. Almost all the girls had their coats confiscated before they arrived in Molidorf. The future did not look very bright for any of them.

The food line kept getting longer as more people came into the camp. The lines quickly turned into mobs, as people pushed and shoved and fought each other to gain a better position in line. Anna learned early on that for her to keep her place in the line, she had to fight or be pushed down onto the ground. The sound of the people clanging their pots against the kettles was almost deafening. The people lost all dignity as they fought to be the next to be served. *Hunger sure brings out the worst in people*, Anna thought.

One day, while Anna was searching for anything to eat behind the houses, she found an empty lard container. She lifted the lid and scraped her fingers along the insides of the can. The lard was old and rancid, but it was something to eat. Another day, while Anna was outside hunting for anything to eat, she heard the sounds of excitement and despair. She determined that the noise was coming from the wooden fence outside the commandant's backyard. Children were fighting over potato peels that were being tossed over the fence by the woman peeling potatoes for the commandant's next meal. She knew the children were there catching the peels, so she made them extra thick.

November rolled by, and Anna continued to wonder what became of the rest of her family. Up until then, her mind was occupied with getting food. She worked up the motivation to go look for her Omas and Little Anna. She ran into a boy she recognized from Setschan. He told her that her brother Stefan was working in the fields when the rest of the townspeople were being forced out of Setschan. Instead of being sent to Molidorf like the rest of his family, Stefan lived in the horse barn back in Setschan and was charged with caring for the soldiers' horses. He did not get any special privileges or extra food while in that service. He was, however, spared the horror of living in the camp.

Reunion with Little Anna

One day, while standing in the food line, Anna heard a familiar voice calling, "Anna Friedrich, is that you?" Anna turned around, and there was Lisle with her daughter and Little Anna. Anna gave up her place in the food line and ran back and put her arms around Little Anna. Both cried as they hugged each other. Little Anna was six years old and very thin. "Is Oma with you?" Little Anna asked.

"No. I think she's still in Setschan," Anna answered.

Anna found out that Lisle, her daughter, and Little Anna lived only a few houses down on the other side on the street. The girls talked until they got to the kettles. The woman serving the soup filled Anna's bowl and then pulled her aside, out of view of the others in line, and gave her a little extra in her pot. Anna recognized the woman as Frau Baumstark from her neighborhood in Setschan. Her son Jakob once had a crush on Anna's sister, Kathi.

Little Anna went to visit her aunt Anna often. They waited in the food line together. They would always get into Frau Baumstark's line. She would reach down to the bottom of the kettle with her ladle, where most of the cornmeal had settled. Because of Frau Baumstark, Anna was the first to get any leftovers. Every day, the people standing in line, in acts of desperation, mobbed the kettles. They would lose half of their soup trying to fight their way out of the unruly crowd.

With the number of people coming into the camp on the rise, so too was the flea and lice infestation. At first, it was just head lice, later progressing to body lice. Practically everyone in the camp was covered with red spots and were constantly scratching themselves. At first, the rat population was low because there was very little food in the camp. That would soon change. People started dying faster than they could be buried. Their dead bodies provided food for the rats.

A coat for Anna

One November afternoon, Anna heard people screaming and running toward the doctor's and commandant's houses. The camp doctor lived in the house next to the commandant. Anna saw soldiers standing on top of a wagon, piled high with clothes. The soldiers were throwing the clothes out into the growing crowd. To survive the coming winter, Anna desperately needed a coat. She pushed her way to the front of the crowd and yelled out to the soldiers, "I need a coat!"

One of the soldiers threw a coat at Anna; but just as she was about to catch it, a taller, much bigger girl reached out in front of her and tried to snatched the coat right out of her hands. "Hey, that was my coat!" Anna demanded. She held on to the coat as if her life depended on it. The two girls were in a tug-of-war over the coat. The other girl let go first, so the coat was Anna's. Anna held that coat close to her chest with both arms as she ran back to her room. It was a man's blue-gray wool coat in a large size, so it hung very loosely on Anna, down past her knees.

Typhus, malaria, dysentery, and other diseases spread to epidemic levels throughout the camp. The infestation of lice and fleas helped spread disease from person to person. Rats were very aggressive, and their numbers increased rapidly. The smell of death permeated the air.

During the rainy season from October through December, the food kitchen was mostly closed due to wet firewood. There was no food during those days. Sometimes, it would rain for three or four days, nonstop, which translated to no food for all those days.

Frau Mueller's only child, Evi, had pneumonia. Dr. Heger, the only doctor in Molidorf, examined her and told her mother that

Evi will either get better after the seventh day or she will die. Later that night, Frau Mueller came into the front room. Some of the girls woke up and heard her say, "My light just went out. I think the worst is over. Her fever is down. I think she is going to be okay." Frau Mueller was in a state of delirium. After a while, she went back to her room and wept deeply. When the girls heard her crying, they knew that Evi had died. The next morning, Frau Mueller wrapped Evi in a piece of clothing and held her until the death wagon came to pick her up. She followed the wagon all the way to the cemetery entrance. She was not allowed into the cemetery. So Frau Mueller stood at the gate and wept.

Winter was approaching, and the temperature outside was plummeting. The only source of heat in the house was the wood-burning oven in the kitchen and front room. That is, if they had wood to burn. Frau Friedrich told all the girls to go outside and gather up any wood they could find. Fences, small brush, fallen branches—anything that would burn.

One morning, after it rained all night, Frau Friedrich burst into the house, excited and out of breath. "I need some strong girls to help me take down a tree." Anna, Leni, Kathi, and Maria went with the frau. The tree was small but looked big to the girls because they had no tools. They started pushing the tree from side to side in hopes of loosening it from the ground. They worked on that tree for hours, rotating the girls to get a fresh go at it. Once they started this process, they couldn't leave it for fear that someone else would lay claim to the tree.

The tree started to lean to one side. Anna climbed up onto the biggest branch and started bouncing while the girls pushed. The tree finally gave way and toppled over, exposing the roots. All the girls pulled on the tree with all their might, hoping to pull it out of the ground—roots and all. They managed to yank the tree out and drag it to the kitchen door. They needed to break some of the top branches off to get it in the door. They got the trunk into the kitchen and pushed as much of it that they could into the oven and supported the root end with stacks of bricks. At first, the tree did not burn very well because it was still wet. Eventually, the tree did provide some heat and lasted many days.

The girls had a bucket in the kitchen that would be placed outside when it rained to catch rainwater. One night, one of the girls said, "What is that noise?" It sounded like water splashing. Frau Friedrich was the first one in the kitchen. Moonlight was pouring in through the kitchen window so they could see inside the bucket. A giant rat had fallen into the water in the bucket and was swimming around, desperately trying to escape a drowning death. Frau Friedrich put the lid on the bucket and asked one of the girls to hand her a brick. She placed the brick on top of the lid to weigh it down. They all went back to their beds and listened to the water splashing for hours. In the morning, they eagerly went into the kitchen to see what happened to the rat. Frau Friedrich opened the lid and pulled out the biggest rat they have ever seen. All the girls cheered. Maria said, laughing, "One down, a thousand more to go."

One of the other girls said, "Should we eat it?"

Anna had learned where Oma Rech was staying, so she went to visit her for the first time since they got to Molidorf over one year ago. They were so happy to see each other. Oma Rech was not well. She was emaciated from malnourishment and as pale as a ghost. Anna sat down next to her, and they both just looked at each other for a long while. Anna remembered going to visit Oma and Opa in their home. Oma always had hot chocolate and cookies or strudel. After her visit with Oma Rech, Anna went to visit Friedrich Oma. She was complaining that there wasn't enough food and that people were stealing from her and each other. Anna's visit with her was short. The room Friedrich Oma was in was dark, and it made Anna feel uneasy.

The quality of their lives sank to the lowest point imaginable. The winter was bitter cold, and still, there was no heat. They stood in long food lines, sometimes for hours in the frigid cold. For many people, life was like a nightmare they couldn't wake up from. The elderly and the very sick that could not endure standing in line in the cold went without food. Many of them died from starvation. Disease was rampant and was killing one out of every four people. The girls gave up keeping count of how many dead bodies were on the death wagons that passed by their window every day on the way to the cemetery.

Several elderly German men were given the job of digging graves and collecting dead bodies. These men would drive their wagons up and down all the streets of the camp every day to collect the dead. When one person in a house died, the other occupants of the house carried the deceased person out to the street to be picked up by the men with the wagons. Once a space inside the house was vacated, someone else living in one of the barns was eager to move into a much warmer, dryer condition inside.

As the body count rose, so did the rat population. People were dying faster than could be hauled off. When that happened, they put the bodies outside on the patio or they stacked them in the barns. At night, the rats were feeding on human body parts, gnawing off the soft tissue around the face and ears that rendered the deceased person unrecognizable. The rats were fearless, standing their ground when someone tried to scare them off. The bodies were naked because someone was always willing to strip the clothes off the dead to keep themselves warm. Sometimes in the morning, when Anna went to get food, she would have to step over some of the bodies lying in the street. She looked down at them, their faces chewed off by rats. She had no more empathy, no feelings of sadness or pain; she was completely desensitized to the horror she was experiencing. Anna was now in full survival mode, and nothing else mattered.

One night, three women from the back room were standing by the kitchen door, whispering to each other while looking out the kitchen window. In the middle of a blistery cold winter night, they saw several women on their knees in front of the commandant's house, smoothing the bumps out of the frozen mud in the street with their bare hands. They learned later that the women were caught sneaking back into camp from a night excursion to a nearby town to beg for food, and this was their punishment.

Sneaking out of the camp was easy. There were no fences with barbed wire, and the number of guards went down to a few at night. The communist soldiers knew that if someone tried to escape, they would be captured. Communist soldiers were everywhere; and the people did not have enough warm clothes, food, or strength to make it very far. The people that did sneak out of camp at night did so with the intention of slipping back in. Those that were caught were punished severely in a variety of ways, with beatings and rape at the top of the list.

Early one January morning, three women were late to roll call. The commandant was already there. He yelled at the women for being late, and as punishment, he ordered the three to lay in the freezing cold water and mud in a drainage ditch along the side of the road. The women were then ordered to walk, in their wet frozen clothes, seven kilometers to Zerne to work a fourteen-hour day.

On the walk back to camp, there was a huge winter blizzard, and one of the women collapsed about halfway back to the camp. The other two almost made it to the camp, but they collapsed from exhaustion about five hundred meters from the camp entrance. People within the camp could hear the two women crying for help, but no one was allowed to give them aid. One of the women did manage to crawl on her belly the rest of the way to the camp. The two that didn't make it back were found the next morning, frozen to death. Both the women that died were from Setschan. They were twenty-five-year-old Theresia Lutz, who left behind one boy, and twenty-eight-year-old Elisabeth Menches, who left behind two children. Years later, the story was reported by one of the local newsprints.

Sparrows

It was snowing one day in January 1946, and the sparrows were migrating through the area on their way south. Frau Friedrich said she had an idea. She said, "Let's go outside and try to catch some sparrows. We'll bring them inside and cook them." The girls had no knowledge of how to catch sparrows. They just knew that they were very fast and difficult to catch.

Frau Friedrich told them to go out to the barn and close the top half of the split door. "Sprinkle some corn bread from the food kitchen on the ground just inside the door and hide behind the bottom half of the door. When there are plenty of sparrows plucking up the corn bread, quickly slam the bottom door closed. The sparrows will render themselves unconscious by flying into the windows or the door when they try to escape." Frau Friedrich showed the girls how to collect the stunned sparrows and to rip off their heads as soon as they picked them up.

Some of the girls went out to the barn and brought back twelve, eighteen, and twenty birds. This made everyone sit up and pay attention. Anna was the last one to go out. To her delight, after waiting a very long time behind the door, she came back with twenty-four sparrows. She couldn't carry all of them, so she made two trips. Frau Friedrich dipped each bird, holding its feet, into very hot water to remove the feathers. Once clean, she boiled them in water. All the girls got three sparrows each. They gobbled down every bit of the birds, bones, feet, and guts.

An infestation of parasites caused all the girls to itch and scratch themselves to the point of bleeding with no relief. The smell of blood attracted more rats. They became more brazen every day, defying the humans by running through the house, even crawling over the people while they slept. The starving people were too weak to chase the rats off.

One day, Frau Friedrich came into the house, out of breath. She said, "Girls, I just saw a cat go up into the attic. Go out there and catch it and kill it. Bring it inside, and we will cook it and eat it." Anna was half asleep and did not respond to the frau's request. Some of the other girls went out to the barn and climbed up into the attic. After a while, they returned to the house and woke up Anna. "You have to help us, Anna. None of us can kill the cat," they said. Anna reluctantly got up and went out to the barn with the girls. She climbed up into the attic and saw a cat hanging from a rope. "Kill it, Anna," said one of the girls. Anna looked around and found a piece of steel pipe. She swung the pipe through the air as hard as she could and whacked the cat cross the neck. Anna didn't remember if she ate any of the cat.

By February 1946, Anna stopped going to the kitchen for food. She wasn't hungry anymore. She was at the point where she didn't feel anything. She stayed in her little stall and slept all day. When she felt the need to urinate, she crawled out of her stall in the front room and stumbled her way to the outhouse. Everything was in a fog. Her eyesight was down to about 20 percent of normal. The seat and walls were covered with feces and dried urine. She squatted on the toilet seat and urinated into the hole. She looked down one day and saw that her urine was a thick brownish jelly-like liquid. She was completely dehydrated. She crawled back to her stall and went back to sleep.

Djurin

Toward the end of February 1946, a woman from the house next door told Frau Friedrich that Maria and another woman from Dr. Heger's office were spraying a pesticide called DDT with one of the communist soldiers. This pesticide proved very effective against the lice and flea infestation but at great cost. History would show that DDT was one of the worst man-made environmental disasters of the twentieth century. Still, the people rejoiced at their bug-free environment.

All the girls were told to clear out so the soldiers could spray the sleeping spaces. Anna crawled to the end of her space. She barely had the strength to crawl over the wood bench and to the brick wall of the oven. She held on to the brick wall to stand up. She managed to walk over to one of the front room windows. She looked out over the snow-covered landscape and realized she had not been outside since the last time she went to the food kitchen about three weeks earlier. The door to the front room suddenly opened. She watched while a soldier in a Serbian uniform sprayed the pesticide and the two women following close behind dusted everything with flea powder. Anna got a closer look at the soldier as he passed by her. She whispered to herself, "I know this man. His name is Djurin." But in her foggy state, she could not remember where she knew him from or if she saw him in a dream.

One of the other girls said he was asking around for the Friedrich family. He was told by another family that the entire Friedrich family was dead. Well, that was not exactly accurate. All of a sudden, Anna remembered where she knew the man from. Djurin was the Serbian bridge builder who, in 1942, rented a room in the Friedrich house. Frau Friedrich took Anna by her shoulders and pushed her to walk up behind Djurin. Anna tapped him on the shoulder. He turned around and gave her a look that said, "How dare you touch me!"

Frau Friedrich asked him if he knew this girl. He looked at Anna, dirty and covered with bug bites on her face. She had lost about thirty pounds. Her hair was matted and full of lice, and her clothes hadn't been washed in over a year. He looked at Anna's face and started to tear up. He said in a choked up voice, "Oh, Hanna." That was what he called her in Setschan. He squatted down to her level and put his arms around her. He whispered in her ear, "I've been looking for you." He offered money to buy food, but Frau Friedrich said there was no place where they could buy any. Djurin continued his job of spraying everyone and everything in the houses with DDT and then left.

The next morning, some of the girls were up early. Looking out the front room window, they saw Djurin walking briskly toward their house. "Anna, Anna, get up. He's coming back," said one of the girls. Anna crawled up onto the wooden bench beside her bed. Djurin came into the house and sat down on the bench next to her. He took from his coat a glass of milk, a piece of bread, and a bar of soap. Anna's eyes opened wide. She had not seen milk or any form of soap for over one year.

Later that same day, Djurin came back to the house and told Frau Friedrich to wait thirty minutes and then send Anna to Dr. Heger's house, right across the street, with a pot of some kind under her coat. Anna crawled out of her space, and Frau Friedrich helped her get ready. Anna was so weak that she could hardly stand up. She hadn't been out of the house for almost one month.

She stepped outside into the bitter cold and walked across the frozen and bumpy street. When she entered the doctor's house, the smell of cooked beans and fresh baked bread filled the air. There were three soldiers sitting at the kitchen table. Anna saw three empty dinner plates and an open bottle of wine on the table. Djurin asked the ranking soldier sitting at the table something in Serbian. Anna did not understand what he asked; she only saw the soldier shrug his shoulders in response, indicating that whatever Djurin asked, it was okay with him.

Djurin knew it was against regulations. Despite the soldier allowing it, the consequences could be harsh for him and Anna. He filled Anna's pot half full of beans and then placed a big piece of bread on top of the beans. He placed the pot back into Anna's shaking hands. Her eyes got big as silver dollars when she looked into the pot. "Danke, danke" was all she could say.

She put the pot and bread under her coat and slowly walked back to her house, being careful not to spill a drop. Frau Friedrich met her at the door and held the pot while Anna removed her coat. She sat down on the bench at the end of the row of bed stalls and began eating the beans and bread. All the girls were standing around, watching her eat. When she was full, which did not take long due to her stomach having shrunk so much, she gave each of the remaining thirteen girls—one of the girls had died that night—one spoonful of beans and a small piece of bread. She offered some to Frau Friedrich; but she said, "No, Anna, that was for you."

Anna never saw Djurin again. He finished his job of spraying insecticides throughout the camp and left with other Serbian soldiers. Frau Friedrich was mad at herself for not taking the money Djurin offered her. She could have used it to trade with one of the people going out to neighboring towns at night begging for food.

At the end of February 1946, Dr. Jenoe Heger, the only doctor in the camp, fled to Romania. His reasons were unclear, but rumor was that he was about to be arrested for false accusations made by some of the soldiers. He feared for his life and ran.

Anna's reflection

It was March of 1946, and the temperature outside began to warm up a bit. Anna was up and walking around, feeling better. She started going to the soup kitchen for food again. Everything was still the same—long waits in line followed by bug soup. One sunny afternoon, Anna was walking down the patio past the kitchen door. She saw her reflection in the glass panes of the door and was shocked at what she saw. She was nothing but skin and bones. Her face was covered with bug bites. She was frightened of her own reflection. She had outgrown her dress and could now see her knees. She wanted to cry, but her body was so dehydrated that tears just wouldn't come out. Anna thought she looked like a walking dead person. She's seen dead people, and she thought she looked just like one of them. She started thinking about her own mortality.

She was thirteen years old, and half of her family had died already. Because she hadn't heard from her mother, father, or brothers Mischi and Juri for a year and a half, she assumed they were all dead too. She had no hope she would get out of there and no hope of ever going back home. Death was all around her, and there was no escape. It was surreal, as if she was in a never-ending nightmare. She knew she would die there. *Everyone will die here, and we'll just be forgotten,* she thought. Everyone in the camp stopped talking to each other. They just didn't have the strength to do anything but sleep most of the day.

On sunny days, Anna would sit outside in the yard on a big rock and soak up the sun. One day, Anna saw what looked like sunflower seeds on the ground, covered with scattered straw. She reached down without getting up from the rock and picked up as many seeds as she could find. She ate them as fast as she found them. She lifted her head up to see if anyone was watching her. She did not want to share the seeds with anyone.

In May, Frau Friedrich announced that everyone was going to get a bath. She used the summer kitchen to heat up water. The girls were ecstatic. It had been well over one year since any of them had a bath. They all took off their clothes and got in line. The girls were a bit puzzled about where the firewood or the bathtub came from. The frau made sure everyone got their turn, one by one, all in the same bathwater. After the bath, they all put the same clothes back on. They had been wearing the same unwashed clothes for over a year and a half. Nevertheless, Anna was starting to feel much better. Her depression had lifted. She knew that it was the grace of God that saved her.

At the end of May 1946, Commandant Danilov Kesic was transferred to Belgrade, and the camp got a new, kinder Commandant. The food got better. They were now getting vegetables like potatoes and cabbage with salt.

Mother's visit

Sometime in June 1946, a woman came looking for Anna at her house to tell her that her mother is at the Main Street gate outside the camp. Anna cried out loud, "Oh my god. My mother is alive! My mother is here!" Anna ran to the gate as fast as her weak legs would carry her.

All the way to the gate, she was chanting to herself, "She's alive! My mother is alive." When she got to the gate, she saw four wagons, each one full of Serb field workers. Her mother was standing on the ground next to one of the wagons. "Mother, mother!" Anna cried out. She wanted to run to her mother, but the guards would not let her out of the camp grounds. Anna's mother said something to one of the soldiers in Serbian. He waved his hand as if to mean, go ahead. Anna threw her arms around her mother and started to cry.

"Shh, shh, look how you have grown," Mother said.

"Oh ja, almost as tall as you," Anna said. Mother asked Anna how she was doing and whether she had seen both Omas. Anna's friend, Nani Focht, had already run to the gate when she heard her mother, Kristina, was there. Mother and Kristina rode in on the same wagon together. Anna and Mother walked over to Kristina and Nani. Mother began to whisper to them, "Listen very carefully to what I am about to tell you. Do you see the wagon behind me? There is a blanket hanging over the seat. When I tell you to go, I want you to climb into the back of the wagon, crawl under the seat, and pull the blanket over you so you are completely hidden. Stay there perfectly still until I tell you it is safe to come out. Kristina, you stay right here with me."

Anna and Nani were not sure what was going on, and Mother didn't have time to explain. Mother was watching the soldiers closely. After a while, the soldiers ignored them and started chatting with each other. As soon as she saw her chance, Mother told Nani, "Go now!" Nani climbed up into the wagon and under the seat. Anna got very excited, waiting for Mother to give her the okay. Instead, Mother turned to Anna and told her to go and tell her mother, Oma Rech, that she wanted to see her and talk to her. Anna ran as fast as she could to get Oma. Anna told her, "Mother is here by the gate, and she wants to see you."

Oma Rech hurried as fast as she could move. As they got closer to the gate, Anna saw that the wagons had turned around and were starting to leave. Mother was still standing there, hoping to embrace her mother once more. Oma was too weak to run. About fifty meters from the gate, Oma fell to her knees, with her hands in the air, "Forgive me, Kathi. Oh, my daughter, my Kathi, please forgive me." Mother had tears in her eyes as she started to walk backwards, still looking at Anna and Oma Rech. The wagons were now in the distance, and Mother had to run to catch up. Anna sat down in the dirt next to Oma, both of them crying. Anna cried because Mother did not take her but instead took Nani. Mother did not know that this would be the last time she would see her mother, Oma Rech, alive.

Losing both Omas

Anna went to visit Oma Rech often. Oma knew she was there but did not speak. Anna just sat, looking around the room. There were seven women living in one room. One day, Anna was visiting Oma, and the woman directly across her just lay there without moving. Anna noticed that there were flies crawling in and out of her nose. She soon realized the motionless woman was dead. Her next visit to see Oma, Anna saw that the dead woman was gone and someone else took her place. On another visit, Anna stopped at the doorway and saw another woman lying in Oma's space. A wave of fear washed over her as one of the other women walked over to Anna and put her arm around her shoulder. "Anna, your Oma got sick. The wagon came and took her to the hospital where she died peacefully a short time later." To this day, Anna remembers that woman and how kind she was.

On one of Anna's visits to Friedrich Oma, she told Anna, "I won't be around much longer. I want you to have my clothes there, hanging on a nail on the wall. I also want you to have my blanket."

Anna looked on the wall and said, "Oma, there are no clothes there."

Oma said, "Ja, ja, there are clothes there."

From across the room, a tiny woman with a squeaky voice said, "I'm taking care of your Oma. Everything belongs to me." Anna saw that the woman was laying on multiple blankets and pillows, high above everyone else in the room. The next time she went to see to see her Oma, her space was empty. The woman with the squeaky voice told Anna that her Oma had died. The woman had laid claim to all of Oma's personal belongings, and she was not about to give any of it up.

As more people were dying, houses were becoming less crowded. In order to maintain control of the prisoners, the soldiers moved them into other houses to consolidate them. Anna found out that the old woman with the squeaky voice was moved into the sum- mer kitchen next to her house. Anna saw her opportunity to reclaim Oma's blanket when the old woman hung all her blankets outside on a fence to air out. One of those blankets was Oma's. Anna became excited and ran into the house to tell Frau Friedrich that she was going to take back Oma's blanket.

All the girls knew about that blanket, and they all supported her. Frau Friedrich told Anna to be careful. Anna ran out to the fence, grabbed the blanket, and ran back into the house. Later, the old woman went outside to collect her blankets and noticed one missing. She cursed and screamed, "Who took my blanket?" She asked all the girls if they saw anyone take her blanket. They all shrugged their shoulders and said no. The old woman never did find out it was Anna that took the blanket. Anna was happy she had at least one memento from Oma.

Mother's return

The workers that were sick and couldn't be moved during the evacuation of Setschan were sent to work in the fields when they were well enough. Included in this group of workers was Mother and Kristina.

In August 1946, a woman came up to Anna's house and told her, "Anna, your mother is at the gate, and she wants to enter the camp." It had been two months since Anna last saw Mother when she came to the Molidorf camp the first time. She ran to the gate but did not see her mother. A woman standing by the gate asked Anna, "Are you looking for that crazy woman that wants to come into the camp when everyone wants to get out?"

"Ja," Anna answered. "The soldiers took her to the guard station," the woman told her. Anna then ran to the guard station and asked the first person she saw near the station if she saw soldiers bring someone in recently. "Ja, the soldiers locked her up in the cellar," the person said. Anna ran to the side of the house and found the cellar window. She saw her mother in the cellar and said to her, "Don't worry, Mother. Nothing will happen to you." Excited to see her mother, Anna ran to get Little Anna. She told Little Anna, "Your

Oma is here. Come with me, and we will go see her."

She grabbed Little Anna's hand, and they both ran to the cellar window of the guard station and talked to Mother. Anna decided to wait there by the station until her mother was released, lest she miss her. She left and went back to her quarters that night, but she returned to the station early the next morning. Mother was released from custody that morning and moved into the back room of the house with Anna and Little Anna.

Mother told Anna that after she recovered from typhus, she was forced to work in the fields in the nearby town of Modosch. She told Stefan, then fifteen, that he was old enough now to take care of himself and that she must go take care of Oma, Anna, and Little Anna. While working in the field one day, Mother fled on foot and made her way to the Molidorf concentration camp.

While in the camp, Mother was required to work during the day but would return to the house every evening. Anna felt reassured with Mother being there.

The rats were becoming a serious problem. They were coming into the rooms at night, ten or more at a time, and they were relentless. One night, Anna was awoken by her mother cursing loudly. There was a huge rat sitting on the chest of the sleeping Little Anna. Mother swiped at it with her hand. The rat jumped and ricocheted off Anna's head before disappearing into a hole at the base of the wall.

Mother and Anna tried to block the holes with broken glass, but the rats just made new holes. Mother decided to look for another room in a different part of the camp. The room they found was close to the food kitchen. Anna wasn't bothered by rats anymore. At this new house, Anna met a young girl named Lisle Brennessel. She was from the neighboring town of Neosin. The two of them became best friends and stayed in touch for years after. Mother's Aunt Rech moved into the back room with them.

A young woman named Frau Hoeflinger was living in the front room with her three small children, ages two, six, and seven. Anna noticed that the two-year-old boy was crying constantly. He was nothing but skin and bones with a distended belly. Frau Hoeflinger gave all her food to the little boy, trying to keep him alive. The frau eventually died of starvation, leaving behind the three children. The two-year-old boy died two days later.

Orphaned children

News spread throughout the camp that the soldiers were going door to door and removing any children whose parents had died. That included Little Anna. Mother said, "Nobody is taking my grandchild away from me. She is mine. She belongs to me!"

Her aunt Rech said from across the room, "If the soldiers come to the house asking, I will tell them."

Mother became furious when she heard that. She got up and stomped over to her aunt. "You'll do what?" Mother screamed at her. Anna saw Mother from the back, screaming and madly swinging her hand from one side to the other. Anna's jaw dropped because she had never seen her mother act that way. When Mother turned around, the backs of her hands were bloody, and blood was running from her aunt Rech's lips. "If you open your mouth, you will wish you were dead," Mother said with fury in her voice.

Mother decided to give Little Anna a new identity by changing her name to Annemarie. When the soldiers came into their house, they demanded to know if there were any orphans in the house. Mother looked over at Aunt Rech who was sitting in the corner with her head down. "No, there are no orphans here," Mother told them. The soldiers went into the front room and took the two surviving children of Frau Hoeflinger with them. The children's father died while fighting for the German Army. The orphaned children were taken to another camp where they were cleaned up, fed well, and put up for adoption with Serbian families.

After the war, in the 1950s, some of the returning fathers who had survived, with the help of the International Red Cross, went looking for their now-grown children. Some of the children were found, but many of them did not recognize their parents nor did they want to go back with them. Being raised in Serbian families, many children forgot much of the German language.

Annemarie Latzkowitsch Friedrich was now Anna's sister. They had no papers to prove that she belonged to the Friedrich family.

Every morning during the summer months, the workers from the camp were ordered by the soldiers to stop by the cemetery on their way to their work site and walk on the graves. The swelling of the dead bodies buried in shallow graves caused the dirt to rise, especially when it was hot. The idea was to pack the dirt back down and smooth it over with their shoes. Occasionally, one of the bloated bodies would rupture, sending a plume of methane gas into the air.

Local farmers would come to the camp and rent some of the camp prisoners to work for them in the fields. Payments went to the commandant of the camp. The farmers had to promise to bring them back. Some of the workers escaped to the Romanian border. The ones that were caught by the soldiers were shot in the head. Most of the farmers were very good to their workers. They gave them food and treated them well. They even gave them extra food to take back to their families back at the camp. Mother was coming back with bread, bacon, soap, clothes, towels, needles, thread, and cloth. Once,

Mother brought back a metal bucket so they were able to wash their own clothes. Other farmers were not so kind. They abused the workers by making them work extralong hours and with very little food.

Mother could speak three languages: German, Hungarian, and Serbian. She was skilled at communicating what she wanted. She was able to talk with the farmers she worked for, which made it easier for them to treat her like a human being.

The conditions within the camp were gradually improving. The new commandant of the camp allowed the prisoners to have better food, clothing handouts, and some privileges. The number of people dying from starvation dramatically dropped.

Winter arrived and, with it, the bitter cold. By now, they all had warm clothes and blankets. They still had no firewood for heat, and freezing temperatures were felt inside the house, evident by the ice in the water bucket. Christmas came and went, and the New Year did not look any more promising than the last two years. The lines for the soup kitchen were still as long as ever. Prisoners waited for several hours sometimes in the bitter cold for a little bit of soup and a piece of bread.

Anna and Annemarie stayed indoors most days, playing games and napping. They only stepped outside to get food. Mother was going to work every day, even when temperatures dropped down into the single digits. She still managed to bring something home every night.

March 1947 was two years since they were driven from their homes in Setschan, and eighteen months in Molidorf. In April, Mother and some other women were working in a field that was right next to a meadow with spring clover growing everywhere. The women decided to go over and pick clover leaves. They were eating them as fast as they were picking them. Some of the women tied their aprons up to form pouches. The soldiers saw the women in the clover meadow and started screaming at them, "Stoj, stoj," but the women did not pay any attention. One of the soldiers ran over to them and started ramming his rifle butt into Mother's back. She went down onto her knees, but she did not give up one clover leaf. Later that evening, some of the women came by to see how Mother was doing. "Nothing broken, just bruises," Mother told them.

At the end of April 1947, the Molidorf concentration camp was being closed. All the prisoners were transferred by cattle train to either Gakowa or Rudolfsgnad concentration camps. Like Molidorf, both of these camps were considered death camps. Anna, Annemarie, and Mother were sent to the Gakowa camp. Like the Molidorf camp, Gakowa had no fences and no barbed wire, just armed soldiers patrolling the perimeter of the camp. The concentration camp at Gakowa was notorious for the torture and killing of the Schwaben Germans in the most horrific ways.

Children were allowed to stay with their parents or relatives. Living under one roof was Mother; Anna; Annemarie; Aunt Nanschi; Mother's sister-in-law; and her son, Anna's cousin, Johann Rech, who had Down syndrome. Aunt Nanschi had a young daughter named Anna Rech, who was sent to Berlin to work as a live-in maid for a wealthy German family. Anna was not required to work because she was the ideal age to take care of small children and other family members while their mothers were out working in the fields. Mother did backbreaking work for more than twelve hours a day. She would start work at six o'clock in the morning and would not get back until seven or eight o'clock in the evening.

One day in July 1947, Anna and a school friend, Herta, were planning to sneak out of the Gakowa camp at night and go to the neighboring town to beg for food. Anna told Mother about the plan, and Mother protested. She knew, though, that Anna was reaching that age when she needed more independence, so she let Anna go. The plan was to pick a house close to the back of the camp where they could run into the brush without being seen.

That night, they met up and went to their chosen location. They waited at the corner of the house until the soldiers were out of sight, then ran a short distance across a grassy field and into the brush. Once clear of the camp, their plan was to walk until they came to a road. They fumbled through the dark for about a half an hour until they came upon the only road there was nearby. They followed the road for several hours, hoping it would lead them to the next town which, they would learn, was about ten kilometers away.

Further down the road, they saw several people walking toward them. Herta suggested that they hide in the cornfield until the strangers passed. As the people got closer, they could see three women and heard them speaking German to each other. The women were from the same camp as Anna and Herta, and they were heading back to camp with food they begged for in a nearby town. Anna and Herta decided not to confront the three women. Instead, they hid in the cornfield for the rest of the night.

At daybreak, Herta woke Anna, and they continued down the road for several hours to the next town. They decided to rest a bit by the roadside before going into town. They came to a water well at the edge of the town, drank some water, and then began knocking on the front doors of nearby houses to beg for food. Some people gave them bread; others gave them fruit or sausage. Some people did not open their doors. They ate all the food they got while begging even though they meant to bring some back to the camp.

On the walk back to camp, they came across five or six men

and three women sitting outside by a garden with a fence around it. The two girls stopped and asked them for food. One of the men that spoke a little German asked the girls where they were coming from. Herta spoke up first and said they were asking people for food. The group of people were about to pick the cherries off three very large cherry trees.

One of the men told the girls he had a deal for them: help them pick cherries, and after that, they would get food. More apprehensive than happy about the deal, the two girls picked up a basket and climbed up into the trees. They spent about three hours picking cherries until Anna and Herta came down from the trees and told the men they must leave. One of the men said, "Not until you finish the job."

"We have to go home. It's getting late. We must get going," Herta told them. One of the women stepped in and barked at the men for being so rude. She then went inside the house and came back out with some sausage and bread. The girls thanked them and left in a hurry.

They walked back along the same road they came on, eating all the sausage and bread along the way. They reached the camp around midnight of the second day. They hoped to use the same way back into the camp, but they could not remember what house they left from. The girls decided to make a run for it. Just then, they heard a voice yell, "Stoj, stoj!" The girls froze. Two soldiers ran up to them and asked them questions in Serbian. Neither girl understood what they were saying, but they did understand his rifle barrel pointing at them.

They walked ahead of the soldier through the streets of the camp until they came to a house the soldiers used as a holding cell. "Stoj!" he yelled at the two girls. He unlocked the front door and shoved the girls into the house and then quickly locked the door behind them. The house was complete dark inside. The girls were tripping over other people on the floor. On their hands and knees, they felt their way to an open spot on the floor and sat down. A short time later, the front door opened, and more people were shoved in. While the door was open, there was enough light to see that the house was crowded with women who were caught trying to sneak back into the camp from a night of begging.

In the morning, the door opened; and a soldier, accompanied by two other soldiers, were yelling at all the detainees to come outside and form a line. The women were escorted to the front door of the commandant's house. One by one, they were called into the house to answer questions about where they went and what they were doing. When it was Anna's turn, the interrogator asked her if there was anyone with her. "No," Anna said.

Then he said, "Don't you know that you could get shot out there? Go back to your house and stay out of trouble." When Anna got home, Mother was waiting by the door. She was crying and said, "I never should have let you go." Anna decided she had had enough adventure for a while.

The brick factory

One morning in late June 1947, Mother and Aunt Nanschi were standing outside, waiting for their work assignments. Two men in a horse-drawn wagon showed up, wanting to rent several people to work in their brick factory. The two men were talking to the commandant in Hungarian. Mother understood what they were talking about and spoke up, "I have experience working in a brick factory." She nudged Aunt Nanschi to raise her hand too. The two of them were selected for the job, along with two young sisters. The four women were told to go back to their houses and collect their things because the job would be lasting two to three weeks. They were also told to bring their children.

Mother and Aunt Nanschi ran back to the house and told Anna, Annemarie, and Johann, to pack all their belongings because they would be going to the brick factory to work. The sisters also ran back to their house to gather their belongings. One of the sisters had an infant. Caring for the baby while the sisters were working was their mother. Anna could not remember their names.

All nine of them—Mother, Anna, Annemarie, Aunt Nanschi, Johann, the two sisters, their mother and the baby—ran back to the wagon as fast as they could, not wanting to miss it. They were told to climb into the back of the wagon and sit on the floor. Mother sat down with Annemarie in her lap and Anna next to her. Two men sat on the bench in the front of the wagon. One of the men looked back at all of them and gave them a reassuring smile. Anna remembered a feeling of elation, like she was being rescued from her nightmare.

As the wagon rolled past the main gate and outside of the camp, Anna became excited and anxious. She wished she could make the horses go faster, away from the camp, before the soldiers changed their minds and called them back.

The ride to the Klopp Family Brick Factory took about three hours. The two men up front driving the wagon were chatting and laughing. It was a beautiful ride through the countryside. The air was clean and fresh with the scent of flowers in bloom all along the road. They passed by people working on farms with fields of corn, wheat, and cabbage. As they drove through different towns, they saw people working in their yards and children playing. It was as if they were untouched by the ravages of war.

Anna fell asleep and didn't wake until they arrived at the brick factory early that afternoon. They saw many bricks drying in the sun. The wagon stopped next to two houses. An old man and two younger men walked up to them and pointed to one of the houses, indicating that they all could move into that house. Mother was now the matriarch of the Friedrich family. Mother, Anna, Annemarie, Aunt Nanschi, and Johan moved into the larger room, while the other three women and their infant moved into the other smaller room. They still had straw for bed, but there were sheets and pillows left from the last group of workers. The old man told them to rest, cook something, and sleep because they were to begin working early the next morning. "There's a garden behind the house. Take what you need," the old man said. Mother went out to the garden and picked enough to make a vegetable stew. The house had a kitchen with pots, dishes, silverware, and spices.

Early the next morning, Mother, Aunt Nanschi, and the sisters, along with the two men from the wagon and two other young men, started working: stacking bricks, mixing the mortar that the bricks were made of, and various other jobs around the factory. Even Johan did his part by carrying water to the workers. The mother of the sisters stayed at the house, caring for the infant. Anna and Annemarie, both too young to work, also stayed at the house, entertaining each other and napping.

They worked long hours, sometimes twelve hours per day. The workers would go home completely covered with dust, the color of which depended on the color of the bricks they were making that day.

The group all showed signs of returning to health. They started gaining weight and feeling stronger. Anna was almost fourteen years old and was developing into a young woman. She got taller and her bust got bigger, which made her dress fit too tight.

Escape from rape

One afternoon in July of 1947, while taking a nap, Anna was awoken by the sound of someone opening the door to her room. Anna looked around for Annemarie, but she was outside. Standing in the opened doorway was one of the older men she remembered seeing when they first arrived at the brick factory. The man had his pants open and was exposing himself. Anna froze with fear.

There was only one door and one open window with no screen. The man closed the door behind him and walked toward Anna as she backed up into the corner of the room. As he got closer, Anna's fight-or-flight instinct kicked in. She lunged at the man, something he did not expect, and pushed him back enough to jump through the open window. She ran over to where Mother was working. "Anna, what is wrong with you?" Mother asked. She didn't know how to tell her Mother what just happened. Anna and Mother never talked about sex before. She saw the same man a few hours later and avoided any contact with him.

Planning their escape

It had been four weeks since they arrived at the brick factory. Anna saw Mother and one of the sisters speaking Hungarian to a strange-looking man who showed up one evening. The man came back several more times in the following days, each time speaking Hungarian to Mother and both sisters.

One evening, Mother called Anna and Annemarie outside to talk. She said, "Now listen to me very carefully." Anna knew Mother's tone to mean, "Pay attention. This is serious." Mother told them, "Tonight, when you go to sleep, leave your clothes and shoes on. When I wake you, be very quiet."

"Why, Mother?" Anna asked.

Mother replied, "Don't ask any questions. Just do what I tell you. I'll explain later." Anna fell asleep wondering what Mother was up to. She was awoken by Mother's hand over Anna's mouth, "Shh, be very quiet. We don't want to wake the men asleep in the other house." Anna and Annemarie went outside. Aunt Nanschi, Johann Rech, the sisters, their mother, and the infant were already waiting outside. The other person present was the Hungarian man Mother had been talking to in secret. Mother had a bundle under her arm. The man motioned to them to follow him. It was around midnight, but light from the moon was enough to see their way.

They walked for about two hours when the Hungarian man stopped and told Mother that was as far as he could go with them. He told Mother that the road would take them to the Hungarian border. He said there should not be any soldiers on the road and that they would be safe. The man went back the same way they came. From that point forward, the group were on their own. They continued down the road, with Johann trying to walk ahead of them.

Mother said with a stern whisper, "Johann, get back and walk with your mother." Johann obeyed everything Mother told him. Mother cautioned everyone to remain quiet. "If we get caught, we will most certainly be sent back to Gakowa, or maybe even get shot," she told them. All of them were confused and afraid, all except Mother. She gave the appearance of being in control although she had no idea where they were going or what their future looked like.

The group walked for about an hour when they heard dogs barking. One of the women said they must be in Hungary by now. Mother was not so sure. She knew that the soldiers used dogs at border crossings. She did not believe they had crossed the border yet. Mother suggested that they all go into the cornfield and wait until it was light out. Mother led the group deep into the cornfield adjacent to the road, where they all sat down in the dirt and waited until daylight. They were exhausted and fell asleep quickly.

They were awoken by the morning sunlight filtering through the tall cornstalks. Mother put her finger to her lips, reminding them to keep quiet. Annemarie was still asleep. Anna wondered what Hungary was like and if the people were friendly. Annemarie awoke and said she needed to urinate. Mother pointed and told her to go over a few rows of cornstalks. They had already consumed what little food and water they brought with them. Mother estimated they would be in Hungary by noon.

Anna started to panic when she heard men's voices nearby. Mother leaned over to Anna and whispered, "I don't think the men are here to take us back to Gakowa. Be still and wait." The voices got louder, then faded. Mother asked Aunt Nanschi to go with her to check out who and where the voices were coming from. They stooped down to avoid being seen and waddled like penguins in the direction of the voices, being very careful not to disturb the corn stalks. When they returned, Mother's smile indicated that everything was fine. "Those men work in the next field," Mother told them. The baby woke up and started crying. Mother told the sister to do whatever it takes to keep her baby quiet. The baby stopped crying as soon as the young mother began breastfeeding.

Having a better idea of what to do, Mother decided that it would be safer if they waited there in the cornfield until the dark of night. By midday, the heat was sweltering and the humidity was stifling. Mother found some half-ripe ears of corn. They all ate some of the corn. To pass the time and take their minds off the heat, Mother suggested, "Anna, why don't you break off some corn and show Annemarie how to make a corn doll, just like I showed you?"

"Okay, Mother," Anna replied. That kept them busy for a few hours.

As evening approached, Mother reminded everyone to avoid shaking the corn stalks while moving around. The men working in the field left. Once again, Mother asked Aunt Nanschi to go with her to check out where they were and where they could cross the Hungarian border. They walked to the end of the cornfield. From there, they saw a big grassy field and some kind of drainage ditch on the other side of the field. "We'll have to make a run for it over the grass and into the ditch," Mother said to Nanschi. When they returned, Mother said that they were still in Yugoslavia. "If we had continued down the same road last night, we would have walked right into the hands of the communist soldiers," Mother said.

"Thank God those dogs saved us," one of the women said.

Mother told everyone her plan. "We will go tonight when the moon is out and we have some light."

The time came for them to move. Mother whispered, "Shh, we don't want to wake up the dogs." Slowly, they made their way through the cornfield, being very careful not to disturb the corn stalks. Everyone was frightened and looked to Mother for reassurance. Anna's heart was pounding from fear and excitement as she held on to Mother's dress with one hand and Annemarie's hand with the other. Mother's calming voice told everyone not to worry, that they would be alright.

When they came to the edge of the cornfield, Mother hesitated for a few minutes. She looked in all directions. Along the edge of the cornfield was a narrow dirt road used by the farmers. Across the road was the grass field. They could see the ditch with a barbed-wire fence straight ahead. Mother picked up Annemarie and held her tight in her arms. Anna held on to Mother's dress. "Okay, let's go," Mother said.

All nine of them ran across the field in single file, with Mother in the lead. All eyes were on Mother as she led them down into the ditch and back up the other side to where the barbed-wire fence was. Mother determined that the barbed-wire fence had to be the Serbian-Hungarian border. Anna prayed they wouldn't be seen by the soldiers. They found a section of the barbed-wire fence that was trampled and looked like it had been used by others to cross the border. Mother was first through the fence; one by one they all followed. Once through the fence, Mother hesitated and looked in every direction before continuing. Once again, they all followed Mother in single file across another grass field and then into the woods. When they were all across the field and well into the woods, they paused for a moment and rejoiced that they made it to freedom. One of the women cried with joy saying, "We're free! We are now in Hungary!

We're free from the concentration camps!"

Anna learned by watching her mother to be a bit more apprehensive. "We're not through the woods yet," Anna whispered to herself. They continued walking through the woods until they came to a road. Mother had to study the road to make sure they went in the right direction.

They walked down the road for what seemed like many kilometers. They were all exhausted and weak from hunger. They walked through the night until daybreak. Luckily, the baby was quiet most of the night. From a high point on the road, they could see a town up ahead. She told everyone to rest there in the grass by the side of the road until daylight before they attempted to enter the town.

The sun came up, and the town came alive with activity. There were people walking in every direction: going to work, children going to school, people going in and out of shops. Men were carrying shovels and rakes over their shoulders to work in the fields, far more comforting than watching soldiers with rifles over their shoulders. Women were carrying sacks of food and water or wine.

As they walked toward town, Mother warned everyone not to talk to anyone. "If the Hungarians approached any of you and start asking questions, just nod like you understand," Mother told them. They came to a water well at the outskirts of town. Everyone had a chance to wash themselves and drink water.

The town they arrived at was called Csátalja in Southern Hungary. Mother told Anna and Annemarie to go door to door and ask for food. Mother taught them some words in Hungarian— "Kérlek, valami ennivalót" or "please, something to eat." The first house they came to, Mother said, "I'll wait here where I can see you. Anna walked up to the door and knocked. Annemarie stood in front of her. A woman opened the door, looked at the two of them, said something in Hungarian, turned around, and closed the door.

Disappointed by their first attempt, the girls turned around and slowly walked away when the door reopened and the woman reappeared. The two girls quickly returned to the front door and the woman gave the girls each a piece of bread and an apple. Encouraged by this success, Anna and Annemarie were eager to go to the next house. By the end of the day, they collected food, money, and clothing from the Hungarian people. Mother started talking to some of the people in Hungarian. She told them where they came from and that Annemarie was an orphan. The nine of them walked together from town to town, sometimes splitting up but always rejoining the group before moving on to the next town. Mother was always asking for directions to Austria.

Sometimes, they were lucky enough to spend the night in someone's backyard or in their barn. They spent many nights sleeping on the ground under a tree. They continued to go door to door, town to town. The group accumulated enough food for all of them to eat fairly well for a few days.

Their health started to improve, and they had renewed vigor. When the weather was good, they walked through two towns in one day. Their ultimate destination was Austria although they were not in a big hurry because they had no idea what Austria was like or even if they would be welcomed there.

The mother of the two sisters often spoke to the rest of the group about splitting up and going their own way. Weeks passed as they continued their trek northward to Austria. They avoided contact with anyone wearing a uniform. They washed themselves and their clothes at water wells. They walked past an apple orchard and stopped to pick some apples.

The group had been walking for over one month, and they believed the Austrian border was not much farther. They stopped at the last town before the border to make plans on how to cross. They wanted to avoid the border gate where soldiers might be patrolling. "We must find another way across. We should rest here until nightfall," Mother said. When it was dark enough, Mother woke everyone and told them it was time to go.

Just as they approached the Austrian border, they heard a man's voice yelling, "Megallas!" (Halt). He was a policeman, asking in Hungarian where they came from and where they were headed. He then ordered all of them to go with him. Mother pleaded with him to let them go. He did not release them; instead, he took them all to the police station. The mother and her two daughters were arguing and saying, "You see, we should have gone our own way. We wouldn't be in this mess right now."

When they got to the station, the policeman told Anna,

Annemarie, and Johann to sit on the wooden benches lining one wall of the hallway. He then opened a door to another room and motioned to Mother, Aunt Nanschi, and the three women to go inside. Anna, Annemarie, and Johann sat on the bench for what seemed like hours, until the door to the room opened and the sisters with their mother came out looking upset, saying, "They're crazy. They wanted us to take our clothes off."

Anna became frightened when she heard that. She took Annemarie's hand and held it tight. Anna's eyes were fixed on the door, waiting for Mother and Aunt Nanschi to come out. When they finally came out, both women looked subdued and very quiet. Mother never talked about the incident, and Anna never knew what happened to her in that room.

All nine of them spent the night on the wooden benches at the police station. There was no food, but there was a bathroom with running water. Early the next morning, a different police offi- cer came and led them to the train station. He would not tell them where they were going as they stood at the station waiting for the train. They began to panic, thinking they were being shipped back to the concentration camp. Hopelessness and despair overcame Anna as she thought about their situation. *We don't have a home. We're living on the streets. We don't belong to any country. We don't own anything but our bodies, and someone else has control over them,* Anna thought as she began to cry. "Anna, you have to be strong, alles wird gut gehen" (everything will be all right), Mother told her.

They waited over an hour for the train to arrive. Before they boarded, Mother asked the police officer again where they were going. He finally answered, "Budapest." The group boarded the pas- senger train along with their police escort. They arrived in Budapest seven hours later. The policeman led them from the train station through the streets of the city until they came to a three-story brick building with bars on all the windows. Anna had never been in a city that big. She had never seen so many cars and high-rise buildings in one place. She was turning in circles trying to look at everything.

They followed the policeman into the building and down a corridor to another set of wooden benches identical to the ones they slept on the night before. They had not eaten in almost two days. The policeman told them to wait there, and then he left. They waited on those benches for hours. It started to get dark outside when another policeman came and told them to follow him. The officer led them to another room where an old man with a huge moustache was sitting behind a wooden desk, looking over his glasses. He said a few things in Hungarian, scribbled some notes, and then asked them where they were from and where they were going. Mother answered all his questions in Hungarian. He then told them to wait outside the room.

As they were waiting, another policeman brought in three young girls, all of them giggling and smiling at the policeman. Anna couldn't help but stare at them. She had never seen anyone dressed like them. They wore short skirts, high-heel shoes with fishnet stockings, and ruby-red lipstick. Across the bench from where they were sitting was a bathroom with no door. The three girls went into the bathroom, took off their clothes, and began washing themselves in the washbowl. Mother told everyone to turn their heads and not look at them. Johann could not help looking at three naked girls, who were screaming and laughing and throwing their wet clothes at each other. The same officer led the three girls to a different room down the hall.

After several hours, a policeman told them to follow him. He led the group up some stairs to the second floor. He opened the door to what appeared to be a bedroom and told the three women, Aunt Nanschi, and Johann go in and find a bed. He then led Mother,

Anna, and Annemarie down the hall to a different bedroom. "You will all get to eat tomorrow morning," the policeman told them. There were about fifteen iron-frame beds with worn-out mattresses, blankets, and pillows. They picked two beds next to each other at the end of the row. Anna sat on one of the beds and wondered why, so late into the night, the lights were on and people were walking around instead of sleeping.

A woman walked over to Mother and asked her where she was from. "Yugoslavia," Mother told her. The woman said she was from Austria and hoped the officers would send her back there. Instead, she had been there for over two months. Anna listened to her and thought, *I could live here for two months. It's not so bad.* They had real beds to sleep in, something Anna had not seen in almost two years, and at least one meal per day.

Anna lay down on the bed alongside Annemarie. She was almost asleep when she sat up abruptly and said, "Something bit me." Annemarie sat up in bed and was scratching herself incessantly. Anna looked at Mother who was sitting on the edge of the bed. Anna told Mother she could not sleep because something kept biting her. Mother said, "Ja, I know. Look under your bed."

Anna looked under the bed and saw hundreds of tiny black bugs called bedbugs. "That's why the lights are on and people are walking around. They sleep during the day because the bedbugs are less active," Mother said. One man lifted the corner of his bed and dropped it on the concrete floor to create a jarring effect. Hundreds of bugs were knocked off onto the floor. The man looked like he was dancing as he tried to step on as many bugs as he could. Mother suggested they do the same and sleep during the day, waking only for meals. They met Aunt Nanschi and Johann the next morning, standing in the food line. They all had the same problem with bedbugs.

On the third day, around noon, they were all called into an office again. Aunt Nanschi, Johann, and the sisters and their mother were already in the office. Also in the office were three teenage boys. A man sitting behind the desk asked for their names. He jotted down some notes and then looked up and said, "You are free to go." They all went back upstairs to gather their belongings when the woman from Austria that was there for months said, "Why are you set free and I have to stay here?"

Mother and her clan started walking through the city. The three teenage boys joined them, and now their group grew to twelve. Budapest was a big city and took them the rest of the day to reach the city limits. As they walked out of the city, Mother told them they would need to beg for food again. Anna and Annemarie walked hand in hand, going from door to door asking for food.

The sisters and their mother and infant told Mother they were going their own way. The three teenage boys also decided to go their own way. The seven of them separated from the group and left for Austria together, leaving Mother, Anna, Annemarie, Aunt Nanschi, and Johan behind.

The kidnapping of Annemarie

Anna and Annemarie knocked on the door of a house they stopped at to beg for food. A young woman answered the door and looked the two girls over from head to toe. Standing behind the girls, at the bottom of the stairs, Mother told the woman in Hungarian that Annemarie lost both her parents. The woman moved closer to the girls and reached out to touch Annemarie's blond hair.

The woman called her husband to come look at the little girl. The woman and her husband attempted to lure Annemarie into the house. "No, no, no," Mother called out as she ran up the stairs. She grabbed Annemarie's hand while the woman held on to the other hand. The two of them played tug-of-war with Annemarie in the middle. Neither one was going to let go until Annemarie began to cry. The woman finally let go of Annemarie's hand. Mother told Anna that the woman and her husband wanted to keep Annemarie. The episode frightened all of them. They started walking much faster to get out of the area.

They walked down a dirt road until Mother noticed an iron fence behind some tall weeds. They walked along the fence until they came to a one-meter opening in the fence. They stepped through the opening and walked up to an open structure with a roof. They saw that the property was a lumberyard that was closed for the night. Mother was feeling a little sick and collapsed to the ground from exhaustion. Anna lay down next to Mother with Annemarie in her arms.

Anna was awoken in the middle of the night by Mother crying out in Hungarian. Just then, Anna felt Annemarie being pulled from her arms. It took Anna a moment to realize what was happening. She jumped up and called Annemarie's name out loud. She looked all over for her but didn't see her. Anna saw two men talking Hungarian to Mother, trying to comfort her. With the help of the streetlight, Anna saw a woman carrying Annemarie and exiting through the opening in the fence.

She started to run after them when one of the men grabbed her arm. Anna screamed at the man and bucked wildly until she freed herself from his grip and ran toward the street. When she reached the street, Annemarie was nowhere to be seen. Anna panicked as she looked in every direction, calling Annemarie's name. Down the street, Anna saw the woman with Annemarie in her arms as they passed under one of the streetlights. Anna ran as fast as she could after them.

She caught up to the woman and jumped out in front of her, forcing her to stop. Anna grabbed Annemarie's arm and wrestled with the woman, both of them yelling at each other until Annemarie started to cry. Anna overpowered the woman and broke Annemarie free from the woman's arms. Not knowing what just happened, Annemarie continued to cry. The two of them ran back to Mother. Anna told Annemarie that the woman and the two men were trying to steal her. If it wasn't for Anna's brave action, they might not have seen Annemarie ever again.

They'd had no food for more than a day. Mother was getting sicker and weaker by the minute. They walked for hours down the same road they were on until they came to a town. Anna knocked on the door of the first house they came to. A gray-haired woman, looking to be in her late sixties, answered the door. Mother asked if she could spare any food and maybe a place to rest. The woman could see that Mother was sick. The old woman gave them some bread and said they could stay in her backyard as long as they needed. There was a covered patio with straw on the ground. She told them about a town carnival planned for the coming weekend. She said they could get food there and maybe even some money. Mother thanked the woman for her kindness.

Later that day, Mother became very sick. Aunt Nanschi said she had a high fever. Anna looked at her mother, who was pale and emaciated. She became frightened, remembering September 27, 1945, when Mother was sick in the hospital with typhus and Anna had to leave her there, not knowing if she would ever see her again.

Aunt Nanschi said she would stay and take care of Mother. She told Anna and Annemarie to go beg for food. Johann Rech was already out begging by himself. The two girls walked through the neighborhood going door to door. They collected food and money. Anna thought, "The people here sure are kind and friendly." She and Annemarie walked past the park where the carnival was being set up. The two girls had never seen anything like it. All the colors of the merry-go-round, the lights, the music playing over a loudspeaker was like a dream to them. People were running in every direction, but they all seemed to have a job to do.

The two girls went back to where Mother and Aunt Nanschi were before it got dark. Anna lay down next to Mother on her bed of straw, listening to the music from the carnival. It took her back to a happier time when they would go to the Weber dance hall and listen to the Draxler Band play. She became sad at the thought of never hearing them play again.

Mother's fever broke during the night, and by morning, she was feeling a bit better. She sat up and ate a little. Aunt Nanschi again volunteered to stay and care for Mother while the rest of them went out to beg for food and money. By Sunday, they had collected more than enough money to purchase five train tickets to the Austrian border. They packed up all their belongings on Monday morning. Mother thanked the old woman for letting them stay in her yard and left.

Train to freedom

The next morning, using the money they collected, they all walked to the train station and purchased tickets to Vienna. When the train arrived, with tickets in hand, they boarded. All five of them were seated together in a private cabin. Anna sat in a window seat. When the train began to move, Anna could hardly contain her excitement. Mother explained her plan for crossing the Austrian border. Because they had no travel documents or passports, they would need to get off the train and cross the border on foot. Anna was afraid something might go wrong again and that they would be shipped back to Budapest, or worse, back to Gakowa concentration camp.

The trip to Vienna took about seven hours. They were almost at the Austrian border when the conductor announced that the train would be stopping at the last town before crossing the border. Mother and the other four stood up and began collecting their belongings with the intention of getting off the train when the ticket collector told them to stay on the train, that they would be safe from now on. Mother spoke with the man in Hungarian. He could tell they were refugees and needed to cross the Austrian border. The man told Mother he would talk to the conductor at the border. They all sat down again and anxiously waited for the train to start up again. As they got closer to the border, Mother could see the conductor walking through the passenger cars and checking passports. When he got to Mother's cabin, he simply walked right by them, giving them a pass to enter Austria. They all breathed a sigh of relief. Mother announced to all of them that they would soon be in Austria. It had been two and a half months from the day they left the concentration camp in Gakowa, Yugoslavia, until that day, August 28, 1947, when they arrived in Vienna, Austria.

Vienna

It was late night when they arrived at the Wien Hauptbahnhof Train Station in Vienna. There were many people running in every direction at the station. There were German refugees from Yugoslavia, as well as Romanian, Hungarian, and Russian refugees who fled the carnage to seek a better life. They were spread out in the station, sitting or sleeping on the floor. Mother found an open space on the floor where they all lay down and fell asleep.

The next morning, Mother and Aunt Nanschi cautiously went outside the station to look around. They were so traumatized by what they had experienced over the last three years that they could not shake their fears of getting caught and sent back to Gakowa.

Nanschi Rech, the wife of Mother's oldest brother Georg, and her son Johann Rech decided to continue on to Germany where her daughter Anna Rech was sent to work as a maid. A few days later, they were at the train station saying goodbye to Aunt Nanschi and Johann. The two of them boarded the train and headed north to Germany.

A new life in Vienna

The Friedrich family had no problem communicating with the Austrian people because the official language spoken in Austria was a dialect of the German language.

Anna spent part of her days watching people at the Vienna train station. As each train arrived, torrents of refugees mobbed the disembarking passengers to beg for money, food, and cigarettes. One day, Anna was watching passengers when a woman approached her and took out of her handbag a colorful silk blouse and handed it to Anna. Her face lit up as she stood there looking at the blouse. She thanked the woman ten times and ran to show Mother. Anna thought the blouse was the most beautiful thing she had ever seen, like it was a gift from God.

There was a Red Cross trailer in the parking lot of the train station. The Red Cross was very helpful in finding jobs and services for people. Mother checked every day to see if there were any jobs for her. One day, when Anna went with Mother to the Red Cross, one of the officials asked how old Anna was. "Almost fourteen," Anna answered.

The assistant told Anna about a young widow with two small children who was looking for a young girl to help her around the house. Mother said it was okay with her. Frau Schmidt was the name Anna was given, along with her address. Mother, Anna, and Annemarie took a streetcar to the address that same day. Anna wore her new silk blouse. When they arrived at the address, Anna knocked on the door and a young woman answered. Anna asked the woman about the sitter job. The young woman looked Anna over from top to bottom. "I don't need anyone right now. But my neighbor, the Zemene family, own a restaurant and need someone right away," she said to Anna.

The Zemene family had just returned from summer vacation and were ready to reopen the restaurant. Frau Schmidt knocked on the neighbor's door. Frau Helen Zemene opened the door. She was about thirty-five years old, wearing a white apron over a black-flow-ered calf-high dress. Her hair was dark brown with streaks of gray, braided and rolled into a bun on top of her head and held together with hairpins.

Frau Zemene had a look of surprise when she saw all of them standing in her doorway. She called her husband who had been working in the cellar. He was a tall man with a slight potbelly and thinning gray hair. He was wearing a white shirt and apron with three-quarter-length lederhosen shorts. Behind him was his young son, also wearing lederhosen shorts and a white shirt.

Anna, Annemarie, and Mother were invited into their home. They followed the woman into the kitchen where she served them coffee and apple strudel. They asked the three of them where they were from. Mother told her an abridged version of their story, not wanting to reveal too much. Frau Zemene told Anna they needed help in the kitchen and in their second-floor apartment. They sat at the kitchen table and talked for a while.

Anna's first job

Anna was hired for the job. She had never held a paying job before. She was both excited and nervous. This was a completely different life for her and her first endeavor without her mother close by. Anna worked every day of the week except Sunday afternoons.

Mother could not find a job that would allow a little girl to come with her. The woman at the Red Cross told Mother she needed to put Annemarie in a day care or an orphanage. Mother struggled with the idea of giving up Annemarie. She saw little other choice. She knew that it was the best thing for Annemarie. She needed a stable home life. Mother put Annemarie in an orphanage on the outskirts of Vienna. This allowed her to take a job as a maid.

The first Sunday that Mother and Anna went to visit Annemarie at the orphanage, she ran to them with open arms. She looked health- ier and cleaner than she ever had before. She had a new dress on, and her hair was combed and pinned back. She looked like a little lady. The next Sunday when they went to visit Annemarie, she was gone. They found out that she had been adopted by a middle-aged couple with no children of their own. Mother was upset because she didn't remember signing any papers releasing Annemarie for adoption.

Anna was three weeks shy of her fourteenth birthday when she would qualify for a work permit. Until then, she had to keep her employment a secret. She was given a room next to the kitchen. The room had a bed, dresser, mirror, washbowl, and water can. She also received a key for the shared bathroom down the hall.

In the following days, Frau Zemene brought Anna clothes, shoes, and stockings. Anna worked in the kitchen with Frau Zemene, preparing food, washing dishes, and cleaning the family's apartment. Their young son Josef worked with his father in their restaurant.

The restaurant was closed on Thursdays to allow them to catch up on cleaning. They also spent part of the day bathing at the local bathhouse. The first time Anna went there, she was surprised to see so many naked people. She was a little shy and intended on bathing with her underwear on. Anna learned that to avoid drawing attention to herself, she had to do what everyone else was doing by showering naked. After their bath, they all went to the local cinema to see a movie.

One day, Frau Helen came into Anna's room and said, "Girl, what is that smell?" She looked down and saw Anna's stockings were standing up in the corner of the room, on their own. She told Anna she needed to wash her feet and stockings every day. She also gave Anna some foot powder.

Anna was paid on the first day of each month. She became like a daughter to the Zemene family. She looked forward to her Sunday afternoons off so she could visit with Mother. Most Sundays, the two would go to visit Annemarie and her new family, the Koprivas. She was now seven years old and starting her first year in school.

Many of the schools that were closed because of the war provided shelter for refugees. Mother found a small room in one of the school shelters. Aunt Kathi, one of Father's sisters, told Mother where Father was living in Germany. What Auntie failed to mention was that Father was living with another woman. Mother made arrangements to travel to Germany to find her husband and bring him back to Vienna with her.

Many men who fought in the war and were separated from their families, thought they had perished in the concentration camps. With no way of knowing what happened to their families, some of the men and women started new lives without their loved ones.

Mother found her husband in Germany. She knew about the

other woman, but she talked Father into going to Vienna anyway. Halfway to Vienna, Father changed his mind and got off the train. He told Mother that he needed to finish some business back in Germany and that he would join her in Vienna later.

A few months after Mother's trip to Germany, Anna was sleeping in her room when she was awoken by the janitor knocking on her door and saying through the door, "There's a man here who wants to see you." Anna opened the door, and standing there in front of her was her father. She screamed with delight, "Father!" She threw her arms around him.

She had not seen her father in over four years. He said he'd been up all night and would like to sleep before he goes to see Mother. Anna told him to lay down in her bed. They talked as Anna got ready for work. Anna heard Frau Zemene walking down the stairs from her second-floor apartment. She opened her bedroom door and said to the frau, "Look who I have in my bed." Frau Zemene's eyes opened wide when Anna said, "It's my father. He's come to be with us."

The frau was relieved to see who it was and said, "Nice to finally meet you. Anna has told me so much about you." Mother did not want to tell Anna the real reason why he didn't come back to Vienna with her.

Annemarie had adapted to her new life. She was fed well, wore clean clothes, and made friends. Anna started visiting Annemarie by herself. She learned how to use the streetcars and navigate around the city. Anna's mother and father both agreed that she had a much better life than they could offer her, so Father signed the adoption papers. Mother told Anna that Annemarie will always be her sister and nothing can take that away.

After one year, Anna quit her job working for the Zemenes and went to work at the local butcher shop. There, she sliced meat for cold cuts, cleaned the shop after closing, and cleaned the butcher's apartment. She was paid well and got free room and board while employed there. The thought of going back to school or to church was furthest from her mind by now. She was fifteen now and considered herself an independent woman. She enjoyed going to the movie theater on Sunday afternoon with some of the girls she met at the school boarding house where Mother and Father lived.

Anna also enjoyed going to Sunday evening dances in the school gymnasium. There was always a band playing, and it reminded her of the Draxler Band. Father never went anywhere without his clarinet, so he was invited to join the band and play for the refugees.

Father's approach

One Sunday afternoon in 1948, Anna was coming back from visiting Annemarie. When she stepped off the streetcar, she saw Father waiting at the station for her. Anna thought it was so nice of him to meet her there. Father put his arm around Anna's waist as they started to walk. He began asking Anna about boys. Anna told him she did not have a boyfriend, but he did not believe her.

He then asked Anna to go to a hotel with him. He said he could help her clear up her pimples. Anna quickly realized that her own father wanted to have sex with her. She broke free from his hold and ran to Mother, hoping for protection. She did not tell Mother about what just happened between her and Father. From that point forward, she never trusted her father again and avoided contact with him. He complained to Mother that his own daughter had no respect for him. Years later, Anna told her mother about what happened on that day. Mother said she had a feeling it was something like that. She told Anna that Father had been keeping company with prostitutes.

In the fall of 1948, Anna was at work in the butcher shop in Vienna when Stefan made a surprise appearance. He was seventeen years old and turning out to be a fine young man. Stefan moved in with Mother and Father and immediately began working in the construction trade with Father.

Stefan's dream was to go to America and start a family of his own. His goal was to save enough money to pay for the airfare to the United States. One day, Father saw where Stefan was hiding his money. He stole some of Stefan's money to spend on prostitutes. When he found out, Stefan became infuriated and announced that he was leaving for America. After obtaining all the documents he needed, Stefan left for the United States in 1950. Anna and Mother were saddened by his departure. A short time later, Mother and Father were divorced. Anna found out later that Father had married a much younger woman. Mother had a difficult time getting over Father and cried for many nights.

Georg Kautner

In the spring of 1949, Anna, then almost sixteen, met Georg Kautner, my father, at the Sunday evening dance at the refugee camp dance hall in Vienna. He made the first move by asking Anna to dance with him. He was so handsome and well-dressed that Anna had to say yes. They danced well together. They met at the Sunday evening dance several more times.

After dancing, they would sit and talk for a while. Anna was beginning to like Georg, who was two years older than her. They started dating more frequently; going to Sunday matinee; and dancing at the military base where Georg lived with his mother, Katharina, and older sister, Josephine. The base had been abandoned by the military and turned into a refugee camp.

The Kautner family was from the city of Bukovac, near the capital of Zagreb, Croatia, then part of Yugoslavia. When Georg was eight years old, his father, my grandfather Stefan Kautner, was killed while trying to protect a family friend from her abusive husband. Georg was the youngest of four siblings. Even though the Kautner family were ethnic Germans, they were spared from the horrors of the concentration camps. They were lucky enough to get out of Yugoslavia early enough to avoid the persecution and cruelty that other Schwaben ethnic German families endured.

Anna was still working at the butcher shop when she became pregnant at the age of nineteen. Anna and Georg were married on December 10, 1952, at the courthouse in Vienna. Anna continued to work for the Schatz family butcher shop until she was eight months pregnant. With the help of the Schatz family, Anna and Georg were able to rent a one-bedroom apartment in a three-story building. Anna got a job as a janitor for the same apartment complex. Georg worked as a tool and die machinist in a Vienna factory.

The Kautner family welcomed the birth of their first child, Helga, on April 23, 1953. In September 1953, Anna became pregnant again. Two months later, she had a miscarriage. Stefan invited the Kautner family to join the Friedrichs in America. The United States was letting refugees from Europe into the country by the thou- sands every day. Stefan paid all their travel expenses. He obtained a work permit from his employer for Georg to work for the same construction company.

With the help of the Catholic Caritas, an international humanitarian organization posted in Vienna aiding refugees, the Kautners began to make arrangements to emigrate permanently to the United States of America. The Caritas suggested that Anna and Georg get married in a Catholic Church. They went to the Breitensee Catholic Church in Vienna and spoke to one of the priests. He wanted to know how much money they wished to spend on the wedding. They told the priest they did not want a big wedding and instead just wanted to be wed in the eyes of God.

April 17, 1955, was the chosen date for the wedding. The priest called in two church attendants to act as witnesses. He led them all to a back room with a cross hanging on the wall and performed the ceremony. Anna returned to the church two weeks later to pick up the marriage certificate and gave a donation of 250 shillings to the church. The priest said to her, "Why didn't you tell me you would donate money? I would have married you at the altar."

Anna became pregnant again; and on August 22, 1955, her second child, Stefan George Kautner, was born. He was a healthy ten pounds and four ounces. He had snow white hair all over his head. He was baptized two weeks later with fifteen-year-old Annemarie as his godmother.

Leaving Vienna

After weeks of preparation, on October 14, 1955, the Kautner family left Vienna, Austria. They left behind Anna's mother, Katharina Friedrich, Annemarie Latzkowitsch Friedrich, Georg's mother Katharina Kautner, and his sister Josephine Kautner. Helga was already two and a half years old, and Stefan was only seven weeks.

Georg had made a basket out of metal and covered it with cloth and padding, just big enough for a seven-week-old baby boy.

With their son Stefan in the basket and Helga in tow, the Kautner family boarded a train in Vienna bound for Munich, Germany. In Munich, they boarded a Lockheed Constellation C-121, a World

War II-era propeller-driven airplane, with seventy-five other passengers, mostly refugees, and departed for New York City. Including a two-hour fuel stop in Reykjavik, Iceland, the entire trip took seventeen hours. They landed at LaGuardia Airport in New York City. After spending what seemed like many hours to get through customs and immigration, they boarded another airplane to Chicago, Illinois, where Anna's brother Stefan was waiting for them.

Stefan had emigrated to Chicago in 1950. By the time the Kautner family arrived in Chicago five years later, Stefan had gotten married and had two children, Anita and Nancy Friedrich. When Stefan first arrived in Chicago, he worked two jobs—construction work during the day, and at night he drove a taxi. In five years, he purchased a home in Chicago and bought a new car for his family.

The Kautners moved in with the Friedrich family for two months. After that, they moved into a basement apartment on Magnolia Avenue in Chicago. Georg worked in the construction trade with Stefan. After several months on the job, he decided to choose a different trade because he did not care for construction work. Instead, Georg found a job in the ornamental steel industry where he learned to weld and work with wrought iron. Anna became a stay-at-home mother: caring for her children, cooking, cleaning, and doing the marketing.

Anna became pregnant again; and on November 22, 1956, Rosemarie Kautner was born. Three months after she gave birth, Anna took a night job at a plastics factory. She had intended to work only long enough to pay back Stefan for the airfare to the United States. Anna and Georg worked opposite shifts, so one of them was always home to care for the children.

In 1958, Stefan, his brother-in-law Bernhardt Heurich, and Georg joined partnership in the purchase of a twelve-unit apartment building on the corner of Jansen Street and Irving Park in Chicago.

The yellow-brick building needed extensive repairs. The Friedrich family moved into one of the apartments, and the Kautner Family moved into another at the opposite end of the building. Stefan had one-half ownership; Bernhardt and Georg each had one-quarter ownership. The plan was to remodel the apartments and, after a few years, sell the building at a profit.

On January 29, 1960, Anna's fourth child Anne Kautner was born. Life was good in the US. There was plenty of work if someone wanted a job. Anna did not work during her pregnancy and went back to being a stay-at-home mom. On February 28, 1961, Anna and Georg became citizens or the United States. For the first time since she was eleven years old, Anna finally felt like she belonged to a country, that she had a home.

Anna's brother Stefan wanted to pay more on the apartment building to pay it off faster, so he and Bernhardt started paying more to the bank than their monthly installments every month. Georg did not earn as much money as the two of them, so he could not afford to pay more. Anna and Georg decided to invite Georg's mother, Katharina Kautner, to move from Vienna to Chicago to live with them and care for their children while Anna went back to work full-time.

Anna got a job at the Northwestern Golf Company in Chicago, cleaning and painting new golf clubs. The three older children were at school during the day while Oma stayed at home with Anne, still not in school.

The apartment building was sold in 1962. The Friedrich family moved into a single-family home on Foster Avenue in a suburb of Chicago. The Kautner family purchased a two-story, two-unit apartment building on Asbury Street in Evanston, Illinois. Three of the children slept in one bedrooms while Oma and Anne slept in the other bedroom. Mom and Dad slept on the sofa bed in the living room.

Anna's life began to change when Oma took charge of the household. Oma was a headstrong woman whose nature was to take charge of everything. She watched the children, disciplined them when necessary, cooked all the meals, and washed all the clothes.

Anna knew she meant well, but Oma stripped her of all her family responsibilities. It was when Oma became demanding and wanted to run the household her way that Anna became annoyed and resentful. Anna voiced her frustrations to Georg, but he couldn't bring himself to say anything to his mother. Anna realized that in order to keep peace in the family, she had to keep her mouth shut and accept everything the way it was. This frustrated Anna even more, and she became depressed, crying almost every day.

Georg drank alcohol as far back as Anna could remember, but with the escalating tension between Anna and Oma, the only way he knew how to cope was to drink. Georg denied that there was anything wrong with the household arrangement. He denied his wife's right to express her concerns. He was resentful of Anna because she couldn't get along with his mother.

His resentment turned to anger, and he yelled at Anna almost daily. Anna was so depressed that she didn't want to go home after work. She took on more hours and sometimes would not get home until after midnight. Anna cried often while at work. She begged her husband to find an apartment for his mother. His response was that he could not throw his mother out. Anna finally couldn't take anymore and gave him an ultimatum—his mother or his wife. One of them had to leave.

Moving out

Out of desperation, Anna left her family and moved into a studio apartment near work. I remember the day my mother left; I was eight years old. It was a Sunday morning, and Georg shuffled all four children into one bedroom and locked the door. We were all excited because we thought Mom and Dad were planning an outing with the family. Instead, the bedroom door opened, and Dad told us to go into the living room, that he and Mom had something to tell us.

In the living room, he told all of us that our mother was moving out. "She was leaving all of us," he told the four of us. Later that same day, Anna packed some personal things into paper grocery bags. Just before she walked out the door, she came to see me in my bedroom.

The room was dark when she sat down on the edge of my bed next to me. My face was in my pillow; I had been crying most of the after- noon. She tried to comfort me and assured me that I would always be her son and that things were going to be fine.

To occupy her mind, Anna took on as many hours as they would give her at work. She felt responsible for breaking up her family. She sank further into depression, sometimes having thoughts of suicide.

After four weeks of self-inflicted heartache, Georg couldn't take it anymore and went looking for Anna. He drove to her apartment and pleaded with her to come home. He said he understood what she was going through. "Things are going to be different from now on," he told Anna. She believed him, so she moved back home with her family.

Things did not get better; they got worse. Georg's drinking increased and, with it, his bad temperament. He directed his anger toward Anna by yelling at her even more. Oma told Anna that she was a terrible mother for leaving her children. Anna's dream of having a family crumbled right before her eyes. She felt as if she was living in a nightmare. She went through a whole range of emotions from sadness, to depression, to anger and desperation.

Anna saw only two ways out of her situation—move out again or commit suicide. She opted for the first choice. Georg agreed that she needed to find herself. He suggested she take the two youngest children, Anne and Rosemarie. The two oldest, Helga and Stevie, would stay with him. Anna rented a one-bedroom apartment near work, and Georg helped her move in.

Single mom

Once settled into their new environment, Anne and Rosemarie went to school by bus, and Anna walked to work each morning. Georg sold the house in Evanston. He and the two children, Helga and Stevie, along with Oma, moved into a two-bedroom apartment on Leland Avenue in Chicago. As ill-tempered as Georg could get, he had an equally kind and loving side that Anna loved and missed.

Anna was now a single mother, raising two young girls by herself. Many times, Anna was asked out on dates by men from work. She dated a few men just to distract her from always thinking about Georg. She continued to work at the golf club factory, sometimes six days a week.

One evening in April 1968, Anna got a call from Helga, then sixteen. She was crying on the phone, telling Anna that Georg, in a drunken rage, threatened to hurt Helga when he got home. Anna didn't know how to comfort Helga, but she did think she should go and talk to him. She knew where the tavern that Georg frequented was located. Anna found him there with his girlfriend, Ann.

Anna sat down at the far end of the bar. Georg noticed her but turned away and ignored her. She could not work up the courage to walk over and confront him. Anna drank two shots of whiskey, one right after the other. Georg and Ann got up and walked out of the tavern. Anna followed them outside. She was paralyzed with fear and said nothing to him while she watched from the sidewalk as they got into Georg's car and drove off without saying a word to Anna.

Anna got into her own car and cried for thirty minutes. Seeing him with his girlfriend, Anna knew she had lost Georg forever. She took off in her car, speeding down the street, with no idea where she was going or what she was going to do. She remembered a place called the Paradise Bar that some girls from work told her about. She drove to the Paradise Bar and walked in the front door.

She looked around and didn't recognize anyone there from work. She sat down at the bar and proceeded to drink shots of whiskey, one right after the other, until she was sufficiently inebriated and couldn't drive home. At around eleven o'clock that evening, three men walked into the bar. Anna recognized one of them as someone she worked with at the golf club factory.

After a while, he came over and started talking to her. He had a very heavy Spanish accent, and his English was broken. He told her that his name was Jesus (pronounced *hay-Zeus*) and that he was a refugee from Cuba. The two of them sat at the bar and talked for a long time, Anna with her German accent and Jesus with his Cuban accent. They laughed for a bit, even danced to a song on the juke box.

By two in the morning, Anna thought she was sober enough to drive herself home. Jesus asked Anna for her phone number. Anna hesitated for a while. She thought about the events of the evening and how desperate she had become, and just when she thought she couldn't take it any longer, a man named "Jesus" walked into her life. *Was this a sign from God?* Anna wondered. She gave Jesus her phone number, got into her car, and drove home.

The next day was Sunday. Jesus called Anna and asked her on a date to see a movie. She told him she had two daughters at home; he told her to bring them along. The four of them went on several more dates: to the park, Lake Michigan, and for a picnic. They told each other their life stories. He told Anna she should let go of Georg and file for a divorce. After being separated from her husband for over three years, Anna finally did file for divorce. Anna and Georg were married for seventeen years. Their divorce was final in April 1969.

Anna's new man

Jesus moved into the apartment with Anna and her daughters. Anna was conflicted about letting him move in, but for some reason, she felt compelled to let it happen. He and Anna agreed to get married; and on March 21, 1970, the two of them wed. They continued to live in Chicago while Anna worked at the golf club factory. In 1971, Anna became pregnant with her fifth child.

Anna called Helga, her oldest daughter, to tell about her pregnancy. During that phone call, Helga told Anna she was also pregnant with her first child. Helga was eighteen years old and still in her senior year of high school. She dropped out of high school and married her high school sweetheart, Mike Demuyt. They welcomed their firstborn child April on March 12, 1972. At age thirty-nine, Anna became a grandmother. One month later, on April 12, 1972, Anna gave birth to a boy they named Eric. They moved to West Palm Beach, Florida, in 1974.

Anne was Anna's fourth child, and she was the darling of the family. She was four years younger than me. In 2005, Anne was diagnosed with ovarian cancer. After chemotherapy treatments, she succumbed to the cancer. On November 13, 2006, Anne Mills Kautner died of ovarian cancer. She was forty-six years old. She was survived by her son, Tommy Mills Jr.

Telling Anna's story

In September 1984, starting in Oxnard, California, I went on a six-week thirteen-thousand-mile drive around the country. One of my stops was to visit my mother in Florida. It was during that visit when my mother and I sat down in the dining room of her home in West Palm Beach that she proceeded to tell me her life story—this story. During my childhood, my mother never spoke to me about her childhood or any part of this story. I sat there mesmerized, listening to her for five hours. I told my mother she needed to write a book about her childhood experiences. She agreed, and I didn't give it another thought.

Anna spent the next few years writing out her story by hand and organizing her memoir. She collected photos, magazine articles, drawings, and testimonials. She wrote down everything she could remember about her life in Yugoslavia. In six years, my mother amassed an eight-inch high stack of documents pertaining to her story. Anna knew she was not proficient enough in the English language to write the story herself.

In 2002, Anna had a chance encounter with a woman from the church she attended regularly in Daytona Beach. The woman, Bea, claimed to have written and published several books, and she expressed an interest in writing Anna's story. Anna agreed and gave Bea all her memoirs and documents. Bea showed great promise about bringing this story to life.

After two years, Bea presented Anna with a few pages of her

writing, which turned out to be more fiction than biographical. Anna was not happy with her work. After two years, Anna had hoped she would have gotten further along. She asked Bea to stop writing and return all her documents. Anna all but gave up on getting her story told. She sat on her story for another four years.

In 2006, I flew to Florida for my sister Anne's funeral. It was during that visit that my mother pitched the idea of me writing her story. At first, I had doubts about my own writing skills. I have always been a numbers person, good at math and science but sucked in English. Eventually, I thought, *How could I not write this story?*

My mother gave me all her notes, memoirs, pictures, magazine articles, and research material. I sat on the material for several more years. I had no idea how to even begin to write this story. I purchased books on how to write biographies. After studying this process for almost two years, I began to write.

At first, progress was very slow. I realized I was missing one key element to writing this story—passion. I needed to feel this story inside me. I made an outline to show the sequence of events in a chronological order. I purchased numerous books of similar stories: stories of World War II atrocities, of the Jewish Holocaust, of concentration camps, and of ethnic cleansing.

I researched the history and politics of the Eastern European countries. I studied historical and modern maps. I saw how borders and names of countries changed throughout history. The most important research I did was on the aftermath of WWII. I researched what happened to the Europeans and especially to ethnic Germans of Eastern Europe after WWII.

The time period between 1944 and 1949 was just as chaotic as the war itself. The cruel and inhumane treatment of the eth- nic German people during this time period was unprecedented.

Retribution and revenge against the ethnic German people for what the Nazi Germans were responsible for went unchecked. Rampant brutality was enacted by the surviving victims of the countries persecuted by the German Reich. It was their turn to watch the German people suffer just as they were made to suffer at the hands of the Nazis.

Full circle

Anna's story had come full circle. It has been thirty years from the moment my mother told me her life story while sitting in the dining room of her home in West Palm Beach, Florida, until this moment. The story follows Anna's life from 1938, when she was five years old, until 1984, when she was fifty-one years old. It took me ten years from the time I began writing in 2006 until I understood the importance of telling this story.

I spent those first ten years trying to appease my mother. The more I told people about my mother's life, the more I realized that very few people knew about what happened in Europe after WWII ended. I understood that this was an important part of world history that needed to be told. The suffering of the ethnic German population after WWII cannot fade away and be forgotten.

About the Author

Stefan George Kautner is the second child born to Anna and Georg Kautner. At age thirteen, when he first applied for a Social Security number, he changed my name to Steven. He was raised in a bilingual household with German as his first lan- guage. He grew up in Chicago, Illinois, until his enlistment into the United States Navy, just weeks after his seventeenth birthday. While in the military, he trained to become an Aviation Electronics Technician, also known as an Avionics Technician or AT. He excelled in this trade and, by the age of eighteen, was maintaining electronic systems on board sophis- ticated Navy jets. After the military, he was employed as an avionics technician for several privately owned avionics companies, working on Cessna, Beechcraft, and Piper aircraft.

By 1984, at age twenty-eight, he had gained enough knowledge, experience, connections, and credentials to start his own avionics sales and repair business. By 2001, after seventeen years of running a business and working one-hundred-hour weeks, he reached burnout. Living in California, his wife, Varida, and he decided to move to Northern Virginia, just outside the Beltway of Washington, DC, to be closer to Varida's relatives, spread out over the northeastern part of the country.

He was offered a very rare opportunity to work as a paid employee for the Smithsonian Institution's National Air and Space Museum in Washington, DC. As a Museum Restoration Specialist, Steven worked at the world-famous Paul E. Garber restoration facility on Silver Hill in Suitland, Maryland. He restored some of the most historically significant and famous aviation artifacts in the world. In 2011, after living in Virginia for over ten years, he and his wife missed California so much that they decided to move back. He terminated his job at the Smithsonian after he was offered a position in Oakland, California, as an Aviation Safety Inspector for the Federal Aviation Administration (FAA). He held this position until he retired in February 2018. He and Varida, along with their pet bird Betty (Betty is a boy) and puppy Mika, live in Silverdale, Washington, right on the Hood Canal.

He never had any children of his own.

A first-time published author, Steven G. Kautner, his inspiration for this book was his mother, Anna Berry, born Anna Friedrich. At eighty-eight years old, this amazing woman remembered every little detail of her childhood right down to the colors of the clothes she wore and the names of her teachers and neighbors. Steven feels compelled to tell this little-known piece of human history. When describing this story to others, he is surprised at how few people know anything about this post-WWII period of history. This is an intensely personal account told to the author by his mother, Anna, who actually lived the journey of this book.

www.ingramcontent.com/pod-product-compliance
Lightning Source LLC
Chambersburg PA
CBHW021105130626
46554CB00002B/545